RIVER OF LIFE,
FEAST OF GRACE

BAPTISM, COMMUNION,
AND DISCIPLESHIP

JENNIFER W. DAVIDSON

JUDSON PRESS
PUBLISHERS SINCE 1824
VALLEY FORGE, PA

River of Life, Feast of Grace: Baptism, Communion, and Discipleship
© 2019 by Judson Press, Valley Forge, PA 19482-0851
All rights reserved.

Judson Press has made every effort to trace the ownership of all quotes. In the event of a question arising from the use of a quote, we regret any error made and will be pleased to make the necessary correction in future printings and editions of this book.

Bible quotations in this volume are from the New Revised Standard Version of the Bible, copyright © 1989 by the Division of Christian Education of the National Council of the Churches of Christ in the United States of America. Used by permission. All rights reserved. And from HOLY BIBLE, New International Version®, NIV®, copyright © 1973, 1978, 1984, 2011 by Biblica Inc. Used by permission. All rights reserved worldwide.

Interior design by Crystal Devine.
Cover design by Wendy Ronga, Hampton Design Group.

Cataloging-in-Publication Data available upon request.
Contact cip@judsonpress.com.

Printed in the U.S.A.
First printing, 2019.

CONTENTS

ACKNOWLEDGMENTS

W HILE IT IS my name that appears on the cover, I have learned it takes a village to write a book. I want to especially thank a small group of faithful friends and colleagues who agreed to serve as advisors on this project, read early drafts, and were willing to be my first interview subjects: Don Ng, Marie Onwubuariri, Marcus Pomeroy, and Khalia Jelks Williams. Thank you for sharing a passion for this work and for keeping me encouraged along the way.

In addition, I am indebted to others who agreed to be interviewed for this project, including Mylinda Baits, Debora Jackson, Joseph Kutter, and Tim Phillips. Your voices give shape and bring vibrancy to the theology found in these pages, and I am truly thankful that the rich diversity of Baptist faith shines through your stories.

I am grateful to those who contributed liturgical resources to this book: Ineda Pearl Adesanya, Sharon R. Fennema, Jean Jeffress, George V. "Tripp" Hudgins III, Erika Marksbury, Don Ng, Sashinungla Pongen, and Paul Schneider.

Thank you to my friends and colleagues who had countless conversations with me about this book, encouraged me to keep going, and some of whose stories appear here as well, especially Robert Robinson, Sharon R. Fennema, Brad Berglund, Rebecca Irwin-Diehl, and Cherri Murphy.

I am grateful to my president, dean, colleagues, and students at American Baptist Seminary of the West. Your love for God and your faithful dedication to your work give me hope.

Thank you to my colleagues and students in the Religion & Practice Department at the Graduate Theological Union, who interacted with some early drafts of this book and asked some probing questions along the way.

Thank you to the Council of Baptist Churches of Northeast India (CBCNEI) and their General Secretary Solomon Rongpi, who provided me an opportunity to give a public lecture on the material included in this book for their Church Leaders' Conference at the WSBAK Mission Centre, Akukuto, Thahekhu in Dimapur, Nagaland.

Thank you to the great teachers in my life who encouraged me and equipped me to pursue what I love. There are too many of you to name, but since this is a book about baptism and communion, I do want to thank Gordon Lathrop. You graciously provided space for me to thrive and you set me on this path with generous blessing. I am also grateful to Anne Yardley, who coached me to the finish line.

And finally, I am thankful to my family who fills my life with love and laughter: my son, Elliot, who shows up occasionally in these pages and brings me joy every day; and my husband, Doug, who is not only my beloved partner but also my editor extraordinaire.

CHAPTER 1

WHY FOCUS ON BAPTISM AND COMMUNION?

Worship is a first-person-plural activity. Participants are called to be aware not only of God's presence, but of each other, and the world.

—John D. Witvliet[1]

IT WAS AFTER Sunday school one morning when I had a conversation with Claire. I had taught that morning's adult class on the topic of communion. Claire was a cradle American Baptist who had faithfully attended church every Sunday for more than sixty years. Of course, she was at church much more often than just Sundays. You could find her volunteering for the children's education programming on Wednesday nights; she sang in the choir; she coordinated all the receptions and church potlucks; she took her turn as adult Sunday school teacher at least once every month. Even so, she marveled to me privately after class that Sunday morning, "I always thought of communion as something that just gets added on to the end of the service once a month. Just something that makes worship longer than usual."

Claire wasn't being flippant. Her gaze was set in the distance as decades of communion services danced before her eyes. I think she felt like she had missed something for all those years. But what that "something" was, that thing

1

that was missing, was still only shadowy and vague to her. She was only beginning to perceive a hint of a deeper, even transformative, meaning in this monthly add-on ritual to the "regular" worship experience.

Most Baptists and other free-church congregations will celebrate the Lord's Supper no more than twelve times a year, on the first Sunday of each month.[2] Services that include baptisms are even less frequent; if churches are fortunate, they might have one or two Sundays a year when baptisms are performed. So why write a book about things that just don't happen all that often?

If we consider frequency to be the primary measure of importance, then that is a very reasonable question. But that's kind of the catch here. Historically, Baptists began celebrating the Lord's Supper less frequently precisely because we valued it so much! The idea was that frequent celebration of the meal ended up cheapening it. How can it be a feast if we practice it every week or even every day? Think about our Thanksgiving Day feasts in November. If we celebrated Thanksgiving every month, or every week, would Thanksgiving really feel like the holiday that it is?

I don't choose the example of Thanksgiving lightly. The word *eucharist* (the term for communion in liturgical traditions) actually means thanksgiving. For Baptists, the infrequent celebration of the meal was intended to heighten the importance of the Lord's Supper.[3]

As a tradition, Baptists were heavily influenced by the minimalist approach of the reformer Ulrich Zwingli so that we started to see the Lord's Supper and baptism as "merely" symbols. We were also shaped by Enlightenment sensibilities that undervalued mystery in favor of that which can be known rationally and scientifically. And we were shaped by the revivalist movement in North America that valued pragmatic approaches to worship and measured success in terms of how many new (or repentant) believers responded to the altar call at the climax of the service. In many Baptist churches, this altar call replaced the weekly communion meal celebrated by our more liturgical sisters and brothers.

Within the modern ecumenical context, as the liturgical renewal movement of the twentieth century and beyond has increasingly emphasized the centrality of the Eucharist for all worship, the free churches' infrequent celebration of communion made their Sunday morning worship seem increasingly like an outlier in Christian tradition. Even the most generous liturgical scholars tended to view weekly worship services that did not incorporate the Lord's Supper as faulty, incomplete, and paltry in comparison to those of other worshiping traditions. Free-church scholars most drawn to the gifts in the liturgical renewal movement soon began recommending weekly communion services for traditions like the American Baptist Churches USA. We will talk more about the frequency of the Lord's Supper later in this book; for now, the important thing to notice is that for many lifelong churchgoers like Claire, the infrequency of communion has not heightened its importance. Rather, it has made communion seem tangential to worship—an addendum, an afterthought.

In this book we will discover together that the worship experiences of baptism and communion are anything but tangential. In fact, these two ordinances are highly crystallized moments of intentional encounter with God in our communities of faith. Liturgical theologian Don Saliers notes that in worship "we discover who we are, but also and primarily, we discover who God is."[4] In other words, what we do in these rituals of baptism and communion shapes how we think about and talk about God, and how we seek to embody the presence of God in a world that is beautiful but broken and heartbreaking.

Communal worship is sometimes the only place people will knowingly encounter God in any given week. It may be the only time in a week when people pray, listen to Scripture read aloud, or think about their lives in connection to the gospel message.[5] Practices like baptism and communion have the potential to draw people into more abundant and affirming ways of life. The way we understand and practice these two Baptist ordinances is worthy of our careful consideration.

THERE IS NO ONE RIGHT WAY

My hope is that you will be better informed and equipped to both create and participate in baptism and communion services after you are finished reading this book. But I can assure you that you won't find this to be a treatise declaring the one-and-only right way to plan, lead, or participate in these rituals. Perhaps the greatest gift of the Baptist tradition in all its many incarnations is the beautiful mosaic of diversity embedded in it. The gift comes with a challenge, though. How do we think about, talk about, and envision these central practices of Baptist worship in ways that are carefully considered and theologically rich, but not coercive, normative, or implicitly judgmental about how "others" do things?

Fortunately, there is biblical precedent for valuing diversity in how we worship! At no point do our Scriptures spell out for us precisely how we should order a worship service, what we ought to say, precisely how we are to pray, what (or even if) we are to sing or play musical instruments. Scripture doesn't even tell us explicitly how to conduct communion or what a baptism service should look like.

Worship is a local experience. It is created by intentionally gathered communities of people who wish to center their hearts, minds, and bodies on the presence of Jesus Christ through the living power of the Holy Spirit for the expression of their adoration, thanksgiving, and hope in God. Worship is locally generated in response to the promise that God has a word for the people today. Worship is spoken in the local language (even if that language occupies only a small pocket within a larger dominant culture) and expresses local needs, struggles, and heartbreaks. Worship happens in the local dress of the people, which sometimes means gorgeous hats and colorful suits, sometimes t-shirts, shorts, and sandals, and sometimes robes or dashiki or longyi. Worship is filled with local music, whether that be praise and worship lyrics displayed on multiple HDTV screens, hymns in an old Baptist hymnal, a congregation-based songbook filled with dog-eared pages, or spirituals and hymns that by their very presence ground the congregation in a gospel of liberation.

So, too, are baptism and communion embodied locally. Baptisms may occur in frigid local lakes or rivers, in deep, warm-water baptisteries behind the pulpit, or in the backyard swimming pool of a church member. The soundtrack of a baptism may include the gentle tones of a church choir singing "Just As I Am," the applause and cheers of the gathered congregation, or the sounds of ocean waves crashing.

Similarly, communion services may include rice cakes, home-baked bread ripped off in hefty hunks, or tiny, perfectly squared white bread piled on a silver communion plate. Depending on the congregation, the Lord's Supper might be presided over by lay people or by only those who were ordained. In one church, communion might be served by deacons decked out in white gloves, white hats, white dresses, or black suits; in another, that kid who just can't sit still in Sunday school (but always ends up cutting paper into tiny shreds beneath a table) might come forward with his mom and then the two of them weave their way around the congregation to distribute the elements. In some congregations, persons always receive communion seated in their pews; in other Baptist congregations, a series of small groups take communion around a single table, large enough for only about twelve folks at a time to receive communion there. The cups might be tiny plastic ones, glass ones in silver trays, or a single chalice shared by everyone. Some local Baptist church practices might even include wine at the table in addition to grape juice.

In this book, I will not make the case for any one of these practices over and against another. Instead, just as I do in my seminary classrooms, I will seek to:

1. encourage readers to pay careful attention to their own worship practices;

2. help readers question and explore the meanings of their worship through biblical and theological reflection;

3. gently expose readers to others' practices in ways that both challenge and illuminate their own;

4. lead readers through a process of identifying the gifts as well as the growing edges of their own worshiping traditions.

These goals will be encouraged by inviting you to spend a few moments gathering your own thoughts, memories, experiences, and assumptions about the topics addressed in each chapter of the book in order to ground the new information in the rich soil of your life. I encourage you to continue asking your own questions, and to explore biblical and theological meanings of communion and baptism that go beyond what will be offered here. In the liturgies included in this book, I hope you will find new ideas and practices that will both illuminate and expand upon what you already do, as well as encouragement to craft your own worship rituals with care and creativity. Through it all, I hope you will grow in your confidence to articulate the gifts and growing edges of your worshiping tradition when it comes to communion and baptism.

As a seminary professor, I always seek ways to make my teaching interactive, inviting contributions from my students. What the classroom setting offers that the book does not is the ability to be in conversation with one another. That's one reason why we have created a companion website (https:// jenniferwdavidson.com/book) for this book as an extension of the ideas, insights, and questions raised here. Through the website, you will be able to write about your own experiences with communion and baptism. You can ask questions of one another. You can be exposed to more liturgies, and maybe contribute your own, if you're so inclined!

This book will not cover it all. But it will invite deep reflection and spark good conversations. And this will lead to a sense of renewal and a rejuvenation of our practices of communion and baptism born out of Baptist commitments and sensibilities.

WHAT TO EXPECT AHEAD

The book begins with a chapter on theology. We start here for several reasons. First, I want to help people understand that theology is not the exclusive domain of academics and Theologians (with a capital T). Theology is something everyone engages in all of the time, whether we realize that or not. Theology is embedded within our experiences of worship—theology is both shaped by worship and gives shape to our worship.

Second, I believe baptism and communion tell us something about who God is and what God desires for us. If this were not the case, then it would not be worth our engaging in these rituals at all, let alone writing or reading a book about them!

Third, God is present and active in baptism and communion. It is not ritualism, magic, or sacramentalism to admit this. Baptism and communion are not only about what we do. We reduce baptism when we claim that it is simply the moment we make public our own decisions to follow Jesus. We reduce communion when we say it is nothing more than our memorial of Jesus' final meal with his disciples. God is present and active in these moments of worship, just as God is present and active when we pray, when we preach or listen to a sermon, and when we raise our voices in song. All of these are actions we take in worship *as well as* moments in which God acts.

At the heart of *River of Life, Feast of Grace* are two main sections, each revolving around one of the metaphors that form the title of the book. Each section takes a similar approach to exploring the topics of baptism and communion. The "River of Life" section begins with two chapters where we will consider a series of theological images that inform our understanding of baptism. In chapter 3 we will discuss baptism as delighting, dying, and birthing; in chapter 4, we consider baptism as belonging, flooding, bathing, and becoming. Through these themes we will explore ways baptism can become for us a transformative invitation to a life of discipleship drenched in grace.

Chapter 5 will lift up specific questions about how we actually perform baptisms and the theological implications that these events embody. We will discuss the potential in understanding baptism as a process rather than an event. We will briefly explore why Baptists do not baptize infants and address related questions for how we might better incorporate children into our community life through rituals such as dedication. We will lift up baptismal classes and recommend embracing affirmations of baptism as a regular practice.

Chapter 6 will offer you some encouragement for crafting your own baptismal liturgies, litanies, and prayers, and will also present examples of baptismal liturgies that intentionally engage the theological themes and practical issues explored in the preceding chapters. In order that this book might itself embody the diversity of Baptists, several contributors have provided their liturgies and resources to this project.

In the second half of the book, "Feast of Grace," we turn our attention to communion. Again, we will focus first on the theological themes that are at the heart of our shared meal practices. Chapters 7 and 8 will explore communion as welcoming, embodying, sustaining, connecting, hoping, remembering, and sending. Through these themes we will explore ways communion can become for us a repeated experience of God's invitation into a sustaining relationship that supports a life of discipleship overflowing with love.

Chapter 9 will take up practical questions once again, as we seek to embody theological commitments in our practice of communion. We will discuss the question of having an open or fenced table, consider the issues surrounding allowing children to receive communion, discuss who presides at the table, and talk about food, allergies, inculturation, and other topics related to how we share the meal together.

Chapter 10 will provide some examples of communion liturgies that will seek to show ways of faithfully incorporating the themes of earlier chapters into our local church practice. Additional liturgies are available on the book's companion website, https://jenniferwdavidson.com/book.

The book concludes with a chapter that highlights the deep connections between baptism and communion. And we will explore the way baptism and communion, grounded in an embodied theology, can open us to a life of faithful discipleship drenched in grace.

Additional resources available on the companion website will provide study guides for churches and seminary classrooms, a course syllabus, suggestions for new members' classes, and questions to guide conversations with youth who are considering baptism.

Let's start the conversation together now!

NOTES

1. John D. Witvliet, "Teaching Worship as a Christian Practice," in *For Life Abundant: Practical Theology, Theological Education, and Christian Ministry*, ed. Dorothy C. Bass and Craig Dykstra (Grand Rapids, MI: Eerdmans, 2008), 121.

2. Of course, as with all things Baptist, there is vast diversity of practices when it comes to the frequency of communion and baptism. Some churches celebrate the Lord's Supper weekly, many celebrate it once a month, and some celebrate it only quarterly.

3. Everett C. Goodwin cautions in *The New Hiscox Guide for Baptist Churches*, "This sacred meal should be scheduled when it has spiritual significance and never when it has no meaning or value to those participating" (Valley Forge, PA: Judson Press, 1995), 143. Norman H. Maring and Winthrop S. Hudson likewise warn, "There are good reasons for observing it each week, but considerations of time make that frequency difficult. Also, there is the risk that something repeated too often may lose its power to speak to us. Probably once each month is a suitable practice." See *A Baptist Manual of Polity and Practice*, rev. ed. (Valley Forge, Judson Press, 1991), 167.

4. Don E. Saliers, *Worship as Theology: Foretaste of Glory Divine* (Nashville: Abingdon Press, 1994), 27.

5. For more about the frequency of Scripture reading see "Frequency of Reading Scripture," Religious Landscape Study, Pew Research Center: Religion & Public Life, http://www.pewforum.org/religious-landscape-study/frequency-of-reading-scripture/.

CHAPTER 2

THEOLOGY MATTERS

Worship is embodied theology.
                              —Christopher J. Ellis[1]

W ORSHIP IS A time when a church community comes together to hear the stories of Scripture, to pray for their own needs and the needs of the world, and to reflect upon their lives in connection to the teachings of Jesus. The way we think about God shapes our worship; and our worship shapes the way we think about God.

Or, to say it another way, theology happens in worship. The theology embodied in a worship service can be hale and hearty, or it can be thin and wan. Either way, there are consequences.

Now I know that the minute I use the word *theology*, some of you may assume this book must be meant for someone else. Do you ever feel like theology is best left to the experts? Have you ever experienced theology done in a way that made you feel like it was too complicated or too out of touch with everyday life? What precisely are we talking about when we use the word *theology*? One of the most basic definitions of theology is derived from breaking down the etymology of the word. In Greek, *theo* means God and *logos* means word. Therefore, we will often hear people say theology is talk about God. From this perspective, theology consists of the words we say about God; theology is the sense we make of God's actions in our world over time.

Another common definition of *theology* has come down to us through the years from the eleventh-century bishop Saint Anselm: theology is *faith seeking understanding*. There is a searching quality to theology that is rooted in our deep need to make meaning out of the events of our world and of our lives, and to ask ourselves where God is in those events. We seek to understand God's presence, God's leading, God's purpose, and God's word.

Theology definitely traffics in words! Many, many words have been spoken and written about theology. Ask any seminary student and she will assure you there are more words written about theology than anyone could ever read! And sometimes those words are so confusing, so esoteric, so academic, and so filled with insider's language (words like soteriology, pneumatology, *wissenschaft*, and ground of being) that many ordinary Christians believe theology is an elitist domain that's mostly intended to maintain exclusive power structures (or put folks to sleep)!

But theology doesn't exist only in these academic terms. The words of theology also show up every week in our worship services—in the words we say to God in our prayers, in the words we use to talk about God in sermons, in the words we say about God's activity in our testimonies, and even in the words we use in our prayer requests through moments like Concerns & Celebrations or Altar Prayer. These words to and about God not only contain our theological perspectives and beliefs, they also simultaneously shape them. When Peter McConnell asks the congregation to pray for his daughter Lisa who just entered rehab, he is saying: "I believe in a God who cares about people who are struggling with opioid addictions." When Auntie Louise Johnson celebrates her grandson's acceptance to Howard University, someone else in the congregation realizes: "We believe in a God who empowers us and wants us to thrive in the world." Theology is what we say about *and what we say to* God.

But would it surprise you to know that theology is *more* than words? Theology is not only what we say about and to God; *theology is also what we do*. One obvious example of *doing theology* is going to church. Many of us go to church because our theology compels us to (even if we never would have said it that way)! We simply understand that we can't live out our Christian commitments completely on our own; we need the encouragement and accountability of other faithful followers in order to keep faith ourselves. Going to church is a way of doing theology.

Going to see a beloved member of the church after he's had surgery is also a form of doing theology. So is bringing a casserole to new parents the week after their baby arrives. So is getting up early Saturday morning to make sandwiches for our houseless neighbors. Calling and writing members of Congress, carrying protest signs about the limitlessness of love, and volunteering at a local literacy program for adults are all examples of doing theology. All of these are ways of enacting an ethic of care that is rooted in who we understand God to be, who we are called to be, and what we understand God desires for us and for others. Small and big, churchy or not—what we do and how we live out our beliefs are theology.

IS THERE A BAPTIST WAY OF DOING THEOLOGY?

No, there isn't a Baptist way of doing theology. But there are definitely Baptist *ways* of doing theology! Baptist approaches to theology are rooted in Baptist distinctives, or as Walter Shurden calls them, the four fragile freedoms (Bible freedom, soul freedom, church freedom, and religious freedom).[2] Therefore, the theologies that flow from Baptist approaches tend to be provisional, collegial, and rooted in local community practices.[3]

First, Baptist theology is *provisional* because of the historic Baptist commitments to Bible freedom and soul freedom.

Baptist theology seeks to faithfully interpret Scripture and the accompanying movement of the Holy Spirit for today's contexts and in today's languages. A Baptist approach to theology maintains that the interpretation of Scripture is an ever-evolving project. Indeed, this commitment is at the heart of why we call ourselves a non-creedal tradition, because no theological formulation holds true for all times, all peoples, and all places. A commitment to maintaining the provisional nature of theology means *every* theology written by a Baptist can be countered by another Baptist! This is a challenge, surely, but ultimately it is a gift, because it keeps humility at the heart of every theological project. A Baptist way of doing theology does not seek to be authoritative (let alone authoritarian) for other ecumenical contexts, but does offer its perspective in full, equal voice spoken with conviction.

Second, Baptist theology is *collegial* because of our commitment to church freedom and the associational principle. For this reason, responsible and robust Baptist theologians intentionally engage with others as they seek to construct their theologies. A Baptist theology may be written by one person, but that person seeks to be accountable to diverse others within the tradition so as not to produce an idiosyncratic theology. A Baptist way of doing theology also seeks to be accountable to a broader ecumenical context, respecting and engaging other Christian traditions as also expressive of the Body of Christ in the world.

Finally, Baptist theology is *rooted in local community practices* because of our commitment to church freedom and, to some extent, religious freedom. Our ecclesiology—that is, our understanding of what it means to be the church—dictates our theology. The local church is the Body of Christ; therefore, we must pay attention to how the Body of Christ is manifest in a local sense. What are congregations doing, and what does that say about what they believe? Central to a Baptist way of doing theology are shared experiences, local traditions, and the stories communities tell about themselves in relation to the biblical witness. Baptist theologian James McClendon writes, "story will transform story."[4] In sharing

13

our stories, we come to share a theology that is uniquely Baptist. A theology rooted in local community practices invites us to sit comfortably in a space of multiplicity, acknowledging that practices in one setting will have different meanings and theological interpretations than practices in another setting. This is a tremendous gift that Baptists bring to broader ecumenical as well as interfaith contexts.

SO WHAT ABOUT A BAPTIST WAY OF DOING LITURGICAL THEOLOGY?

If Baptist approaches to doing theology tend to be provisional, collegial, and rooted in local community practices, then what implications does that have for how we engage in constructing theologies in connection to worship? For Baptists, a theology of worship—or "liturgical theology"—understands itself as being part of an ongoing dialogue, is intentionally informed by many voices and perspectives, and talks about actual worship experiences.[5]

First, if Baptist theology is provisional, this means our theologies of worship are offered as part of an ongoing dialogue, or as I like to call it, an ongoing *multilogue*, because it moves in multiple directions at once and includes multiple voices. A Baptist liturgical theology is more conversational in tone than it is authoritative in tone. My hope is that this book will contribute to an ongoing conversation about how what we do in worship shapes what we believe—and your responses to it are also part of that conversation. That's why I urge you to reflect on your own beliefs and practices. I also encourage you to gather in small groups to foster dialogue about the ideas offered here. What resonates with you? What doesn't resonate? What would you say differently and why? Where might you be invited to grow? How might you advance the ideas you encounter here through your own experience or scholarship?

Second, if Baptist theology is collegial, then a Baptist liturgical theology must be shaped by many voices and perspectives. From the time I began writing this book, I gathered around me a small group of diverse, trusted advisors who agreed to dialogue with me about the theology I was in the midst of creating. They shared their own experiences of baptism and communion and their hopes for what a book like this could be. They helped to generate a more robust theology than I could have created on my own. Beyond the advisory group, I interviewed about a dozen people, both lay and ordained, incorporating their experiences, questions, and insights into the theology under construction here. Ultimately, the way I have pieced together these voices means that the worship theology I offer here is mine, but it is communally shaped; this is not a solitary theology of worship.

Finally, if Baptist theology is rooted in local community practices, this means a Baptist theology of worship will be talking about actual worship experiences. A Baptist liturgical theology ought not speak of idealized worship for the simple reason that such worship does not exist on this side of the veil.[6] In fact, idealizing worship is the best way to create dissatisfied worshipers. Worship is a messy, human endeavor that sometimes ushers us into an experience of transcendence. But focusing only on those transcendent moments obscures all the many quotidian ones that surround and lead up to them: the water goes up the nose of the one being baptized; the bread is too dense to tear in two pieces. This, too, is a part of our worship. An honest focus on actual worship experiences creates a spirit of invitation for you to step out of overly comfortable places and experiment with your own worship. It encourages worshipers to reflect on and take seriously their own transcendent *and* quotidian moments in worship. It can help free us (we Baptists are free-church[7] after all!) to make mistakes in worship while trusting that it all happens in the context of God's grace.

MANY VOICES, MANY MEANINGS

In the pages to come, we will unpack some of that theology by exploring themes that have shaped people's understandings of both baptism and communion over time. We've already talked about why a Baptist approach to theology must include multiple voices. Yet it may seem strange to some of us (and natural to others) that when we talk about rituals like baptism and communion, we also talk about *multiple meanings*. These worship experiences don't have one and only one meaning, and they never have. The interesting thing is that this is true for the Christian faith as a whole, but it is also true for each individual Christian.

For example, if you were baptized when you were eight years old, how did you understand what you were doing at the time? What words would you have used to describe what you were doing and why? If you are now fifty years old, has your understanding of the meaning of your baptism changed through the years? Do you use different words to describe its meaning now? Do different themes speak to you in light of your life's experiences that you never could have anticipated when you were eight?

Theology, Christian tradition, and Scripture itself do not tie baptism and communion down to a single meaning. Baptism and communion are living rituals that are responsive to our lives of faith (and that includes our moments of doubt)! So the upcoming chapters won't describe to you The Meaning of Baptism or The Meaning of Communion. Rather, they will offer multiple perspectives and entry points.

Here are several suggestions for how you can engage in these multiple meanings so you don't become overwhelmed or confused. First, as you read pay attention to what resonates for you the most. Which theme just makes sense for you? When do you find yourself saying, "Oh, of course!" This is your **home theology** of baptism (or later, of communion)—the place where you feel most comfortable and at ease.

Second, pay attention to what troubles or disturbs you the most. Where do you experience a sense of resistance or even anxiety? What do you feel you might be holding at arm's length? This is your **growth theology** of baptism—the theme in which you feel most uncomfortable and most challenged by. This may be your invitation to expand your thinking.

Third, look for what has been most meaningful to you over different times in your faith journey. What themes speak to you as you reflect back over time? Are there themes that you used to draw on quite a bit, but that no longer carry quite the same power for you? This is your **journey theology** of baptism—the themes that have informed your faith over time. Paying attention to your journey theology is a good way to notice how God has spoken to you through the years.

Finally, choose a theme to explore more deeply for a season. You may want to choose whatever theme you identified as your growth theology, but not necessarily. Maybe you want to deepen your understanding of your home theology. Or maybe you want to reflect on and maybe even write about your journey theology. Or maybe there is a theme that doesn't shimmer or repel but you just want to know more about it—then explore that one. This will be your **focus theology**. Look for a book on the topic. Read Scriptures that connect to the theme. Ask others about their own experiences of that theme. And pay attention to what happens for you as you deepen your understanding.

NOTES

1. Christopher J. Ellis, *Gathering: A Theology and Spirituality of Worship in Free Church Tradition* (London: SCM Press, 2004), 2.

2. See Walter B. Shurden, *The Baptist Identity: Four Fragile Freedoms* (Macon, GA: Smyth and Helwys Publishing, Inc., 1993), and *The Life of Baptists in the Life of the World: Eighty Years of the Baptist World Alliance* (Nashville: Broadman Press, 1985).

3. I owe much in this section to an essay written by British Baptist theologian Brian Haymes titled "Theology and Baptist Identity" in *Doing Theology in a Baptist Way*, ed. Paul S. Fiddes, 1–5 (Oxford: Whitley Publications, 2000). Haymes suggests that "Baptist distinctives do imply a way of doing theology" which he expresses in terms of four interrelated affirmations, namely, that a Baptist approach to theology is continuously renewed and remade, collegial in formation and practice, informed through biblical narrative and lived experience, and provisional or tentative, and thereby marked by plurality and multivocality.

4. See James Wm. McClendon, Jr., *Ethics*, vol. 1 of *Systematic Theology* (Nashville: Abingdon Press, 1986), 31–35.

5. I have written in similar ways about Baptist liturgical theology in the chapter "Contemporary Liturgical Resources," in *Sources of Light: Resources for Baptist Churches Practicing Theology*, ed. Steven R. Harmon and Amy L. Chilton (Macon, GA: Mercer University Press, 2019).

6. John D. Witvliet speaks of the temptation "to give all our attention to the grandest examples we can find" when talking about worship. "Yet this feels a bit like playing a video of Kobe Bryant [or Steph Curry] at a fifth-grade basketball camp: it's inspiring, but not representative or necessarily helpful. Part of the move toward concreteness must also be a move into the ordinary" (130). See "Teaching Worship

as a Christian Practice," in *For Life Abundant: Practical Theology, Theological Education, and Christian Ministry*, ed. Dorothy C. Bass and Craig Dykstra (Grand Rapids, MI: Wm. B. Eerdmans, 2008), 116–148.

7. *Free church* is a term used in liturgical studies to help distinguish between churches that follow a centrally and/or historically established order of worship (so-called liturgical churches) and those churches that are free to change up how they order their worship at any given time, whether they actually do so or not. Examples of liturgical churches would be Roman Catholic, Episcopalian, and Lutheran churches. Examples of free churches would be Pentecostal, United Church of Christ, and American Baptist churches. Evangelical liturgical scholar Melanie Ross does a marvelous job of examining the divisions between these traditions and focusing on the common ground in her book *Evangelical Versus Liturgical? Defying a Dichotomy* (Grand Rapids, MI: Eerdmans, 2014).

RIVER OF LIFE

CHAPTER 3

BAPTISM AS DELIGHTING, DYING, AND BIRTHING

However far the stream flows, it never forgets its
source.

—Yoruba proverb[1]

MOST OF THE people I interviewed for this book talked about baptism as *the most embodied experience of worship life.* It is an astounding, public act in the middle of worship that involves most, if not all, of the senses. Stepping into a pool of water, or the currents of a local river, or the undulating waves of an ocean, the whole body is engaged in this moment. Water rushes over our heads, sometimes goes up our noses and into our throats with a stinging surprise, a pastor's hands hold onto us by our backs and around our arms, our breath pauses, our eyes close or sometimes stay open with a rush of terror, the sound of water and muffled voices or music comes into our ears, our breath returns, the water pours down from our soaking heads, maybe we thrash a bit or have to recover our footing, we smell the scent of a candle, we hear the congregation singing, we might hear clapping or even laughter, our nose runs, the pastor's fingers are cool to the touch and a little wrinkly.

These are our baptism—and they are soaked through with theology. In this chapter and the one that follows, we will explore a variety of ways baptism has been understood over time. Let's wade into the water . . .

DELIGHTING

I stood waiting by the elevator at American Baptist Seminary of the West during a recent all-class reunion. An ancient-looking man approached me, moving slowly with the help of a walker. He was 90 years old, his body not as spry as it used to be, but his mind still nimble and curious. He was a graduate of the seminary back in 1957, when it was known as Berkeley Baptist Divinity School. The two of us stood side-by-side as he told me a story that I'll never forget.

"I used to have an office on the second floor of this building," he began. The year after he completed seminary, he had worked for the denomination, which in 1958 kept offices in this Julia-Morgan-designed building. He gazed up the steps and laughed, "I almost broke my neck running down those steps one day after lunch. I had just gotten a phone call. My wife and I had been waiting to adopt a child. They called me and said there was a baby girl for us, and I could come in and meet her. I couldn't believe it! All this time waiting, and now I could finally meet our daughter! I barreled down those steps faster than my feet could carry me. I was going to meet my daughter for the first time, and I was overcome with joy."

Suddenly, a stairway that had been just an ordinary part of my everyday life was transformed by his story. This now old man, who moves ever so slowly and vulnerably, became a fleet-footed young man—like the one described in Song of Solomon "leaping upon the mountains, bounding over the hills . . . like a gazelle or a young stag" (2:8-9)—bounding down the steps on his way to becoming a father for the first time.

"I will never see those steps in the same way again," I promised him. "Your memory has now become my memory. And I will cherish that."

This memory comes flooding back to me as I think about Jesus' baptism. Like that newly minted father ready to greet his daughter for the first time, the Holy Spirit comes bounding out of heaven, not a gazelle this time but a dove, bursting from the sky, delighting in a river-soaked Jesus: "This is my Son, the Beloved, with whom I am well pleased" (Matthew 3:17).

Some have suggested that the phrasing in Matthew is meant to be reminiscent of a similar moment in the book of Isaiah: "Here is my servant, whom I uphold, my chosen, in whom my soul delights; I have put my spirit upon him; he will bring forth justice to the nations" (42:1).[2] In both instances, God's delight thrills forth. In the Gospel of Mark, God's reverberating joy is enough to tear apart the very heavens themselves as the Spirit soars through the sky in the form of a dove.

Mylinda Baits is a global servant with International Ministries of American Baptist Churches USA. She served for 12 years in Costa Rica with her husband and ministry partner, Gary. She currently trains internationally with the American Baptist Churches in partnership with First Aid Arts to provide hope-infused, trauma-informed, expressive arts-based healing resources for recovery and resilience. For Mylinda, baptism is the moment in which we are awash in the love of God. "We are invited to hear the words: *You are beloved*," she says. "And you have purpose. And that doesn't mean that out of your belovedness you are entitled. It means that you see the belovedness of those around you. You are invited into this community of beloveds." Mylinda laughed as a realization flooded over her: "The Beloved Community! Yeah! That's transformative. And it gives us a sense of hope—that we are beloved, we are invited, and we see our connection to one another."

So we begin our theological reflections on the meanings of baptism with this thrilling image. We have every reason to hope, indeed to believe, that God meets every newly baptized person with similar delight. Let me put that even more personally: When *you* were baptized, God delighted *in you!* Like the prodigal father who welcomed his son home with open arms and a giant party, like the woman who turned over her house until she found her lost coin, so God's Spirit thrills

BAPTISM AS RESOURCE FOR TRAUMA RESILIENCY

Mylinda Baits is an American Baptist who works with communities to develop recovery and resiliency resources in the face of trauma. She helps us see how baptism itself can be a resource when we are recovering from trauma.

"If we understand trauma to be a shock or wound accompanied by feelings of overwhelm that affects us emotionally, spiritually, psychologically, and relationally, then we know it is something that can profoundly disconnect us from others. Trauma, whether it is communal, individual, or generational, is a break, a rupture, a tear. It is so painful because what we long for, and even what we expect, is *shalom*, or wholeness, or healing—a sense of being put together.

"So in terms of a resource for resiliency, baptism has all of the components: it is an embodied act that incorporates physical, spiritual, emotional, and relational mending both individually and communally. Trauma affects all of those areas, and baptism—*and our memory of it*—as a creative act can be a symbol of the healing of rupture.

"Baptism, like any memorial, is a story-holder. It's something that reminds us of who we are, whose we are, and what we are about. It

when the waters of baptism receive you. In this moment, you are adopted as one of God's very own to be in a community of beloved ones.

DYING

"I would like to do more reflection on the idea of dying to self," Marie Onwubuariri mused with me one afternoon. Marie is the executive minister of the American Baptist Churches of Wisconsin and co-editor of the book *Trouble the Water: A Christian Resource for the Work of Racial Justice.* She brings to her pastoral work an expertise in intercultural relations and has developed resources for leaders to cultivate their spiritual capacity for that difficult work. "Dying to self particularly interests me because of my work in cultural negotiation, in the sense of asking what we are willing to let go of when we encounter another's culture. In this work we are constantly dying to our comforts or preferences and rising again to another way of being."

also reminds us, like any other memorial, of the pain of the not-yet—the pain of that which is broken. Like the Vietnam War Memorial. You see all the names, and you reach out and touch them, and they remind you that war separates us. It reminds you of the pain of death so that you don't do it again. Baptism reminds us of Jesus' own baptism, but also of his trauma in his sham trial and violent crucifixion. When we feel overwhelmed with feelings of isolation and disconnection—the feeling that nobody gets it—those are the places where trauma and wounding can be death.

"But baptism also reminds us that God doesn't desire violence and traumatic disconnection. We can look to our baptism to remember that God intends us to form communities where we feel connected, supported, and like we have people in our corner. When we have that, we are able to walk through really hard things and not be traumatized by them—or recover from them sooner.

"Baptism and communion both remind us that *shalom* existed from the start, and that which is broken will be mended. They help us to live into shalom, to live into the connectedness that God intends."

Baptism is about dying. How's that for a conversation stopper at your next dinner party? We don't like to talk about death in general. We avoid thinking about our own deaths in particular. We put off important things like wills, end-of-life health directives, estate planning, and funeral plans precisely because we don't want to think about death.

At the same time, we are surrounded by death. The threat and fear of death is at the heart of the terrorist narrative *and* its accompanying homeland security narrative. We fear death, so we increase security and give away freedom, privacy, and shampoo bottles at TSA security checkpoints. We consume our fears and anxieties around death by putting it on display for entertainment in violent movies, television shows, and video games. We pretend war itself is now only a high-tech video game with drone strikes sanitizing carnage somehow.

Do you think God is surprised by our paradoxical avoidance of death even as we steep ourselves in it? If you think God is surprised, then go ahead and read a few chapters from the book of Judges. Any of them will work. Do it now. I'll wait . . .

God knows that human beings are irresistibly drawn to death and repulsed by it. "There is nothing new under the sun," the author of Ecclesiastes reminds us (1:9). God knows that death and our avoidance of it propels us to do some pretty terrible things sometimes. And God knows the over-whelming power of state-sponsored terrorism that took the form of a Roman cross. God knows that when a government can convince us it has power over life and death, then that government can crush and intimidate people into obedience. So God gave us baptism.

God invited us into our deepest fears, invited us in bap-tism to participate in an act intended to evoke the very same state-sponsored terrorism that killed Jesus. "Do you not know that all of us who have been baptized into Christ Jesus were baptized into his death?" asks Paul in his letter to the Romans (6:3). Not enough time had passed since Jesus' crucifixion for the Romans to have been able to sanitize and prettify Paul's meaning. Your baptism is your willing participation in the worst that this world could do to life, to love, to the presence of God-with-Us. It is truly nothing less than that. Paul is not romanticizing death in this passage, nor is he pretending it doesn't exist. He is bringing our gaze squarely to the cross through the image of baptism. In fact, when we see a baptis-tery, we are also to see a tomb. "Therefore," Paul goes on, "we have been buried with him by baptism into death" (6:4a).

How is this possibly good news? And who in the world would ever desire it? Well, let's take a step back from death for a moment and just think about fear. Think about some-thing you have been afraid of, but that you had the courage to face. It doesn't have to be a tremendous example, it can be quite ordinary. Were you afraid of monsters as a kid, but had the courage to look under your bed anyway (as long as Mom was by your side, maybe)? Afraid to fly, but took that trip across country to see your grandson get married? Were you afraid of public speaking, but made a presentation at work? Were you afraid to call your senator, but dialed the number anyway and read a script with shaking voice?

Every year we vacation with my husband's family in Ocean City, NJ. For the last couple of decades, we have watched from the shoreline each summer as people have floated by in the sky above the ocean, pulled along behind a speedboat while suspended from giant parachutes soaring hundreds of feet above us. Terribly afraid of heights, Doug would shake his head at the crazy things people will do in the name of fun. "You could never get me up there," he would say. And then one year, he changed his mind. "I'm going to do that next summer on my fiftieth birthday—if you'll do it with me," he said. How could I refuse? It was a fiftieth birthday request!

The year went by, and every now and then he would bring it up. "We're gonna go parasailing next summer, right?" he'd say, his eyes dancing with a mixture of fear and adventure. "We're doing it!" I'd reply enthusiastically.

Our week in Ocean City arrived, and for the first few days we watched the parasailers with more interest than ever. They never looked so high up in the sky as they did that year. In fact, it looked like the biplanes dragging banners behind them got awfully close to the parachutes! And when we would see the parachutes drop precipitously toward the ocean as the speedboats slowed nearly to a stop, dipping the people into the ocean waters to drench them before lifting them again into the sky at terrible speeds, our hearts skipped a beat as we imagined our own fate just days away.

It was only after we were strapped in to begin our flight that I admitted to him that I was afraid, too. His eyes grew even bigger than usual, "What? I wouldn't have made us do this if I thought you were afraid, too!" I knew that, of course. Which is why I kept it to myself.

And then we were flying. It was just like that. The boat sped up, the parachute caught the wind, the ocean receded from below us, the sky opened up, the shoreline suddenly came into view, I found myself singing "Happy Birthday," and we laughed. I mean, we laughed like we hadn't laughed in years. And Doug's smile was as big as I'd ever thought possible. And it was silent in the sky, and peaceful. And our fears began to take flight, too. And soon enough, they disappeared altogether as we gave into the joy of a new experience.

Confronting our fears releases an energy and zest for life like nothing else I've ever experienced. When we do the thing we thought might destroy us, we realize it no longer has power over us. We are released from bondage to it. We experience a freedom like no other. We are brought into new life.

This is why being buried with Christ in baptism is good news. This is why we can celebrate when we see the baptismal pool as our tombs. This is why God's invitation to participate in the gruesome death of Jesus with all its associations with state-sponsored terror and imperialistic, totalitarian control is astoundingly, paradoxically, an invitation to life. Because through baptism, God reminds us that despite all evidence to the contrary, it is God who has control over life and death, not the state. And God's intention for us is *always* life.

When we participate in Jesus' death and burial through baptism, we are confronting our greatest fear, and therefore we are releasing an energy and zest for life that is truly without comparison. Because just as we are buried with Jesus in waters of baptism, so we are raised! "For if we have been united with him in a death like his, we will certainly be united with him in a resurrection like his" (Romans 6:5). And if we have confronted this fear, if we have participated in death and come out the other side, then what have we left to fear? Well, to begin with, certainly not death. Nor life. Nor angels or rulers. We don't have to fear things present or things to come. We don't have to fear powers. And, come to mention it, we don't need to be afraid of heights. Or depths, for that matter. Nothing else in creation ought to cause us fear. Because we realize, from the watery depths of our being, that *nothing* will be able to separate us from the love of God in Christ Jesus our Lord.[3]

Baptism is about death. Oh, and resurrection. And that makes us free to confront death, to name it, and to stand against its forces without fear.

BIRTHING

It was the middle of the night, although the hospital room remained as bright as when we had first arrived at noon. My friend Trish had been in labor for about twelve hours at that point. She had gotten up from the bed to walk around a bit and to see if walking would help move things along. Her labor was going frustratingly slowly. Lots of pain, sure. But not lots of progress. Her mom and husband had just left the hospital room to take a quick break, but I stayed to keep Trish company. Her spirits were upbeat despite the hours of hard work, and she was chatting amiably when suddenly she stopped talking midsentence. We heard a distinctive *splash*. Trish's mouth formed into an oval, and her hand shot up to her face. "What just happened?!" she squealed.

"Your water broke!" I nearly shouted. And the two of us burst out laughing with abandon. I can't really explain the laughter. (Nor was I looking to explain it at the moment. We couldn't speak for a long time afterward as laughter had doubled us over.) It was a moment of complete joy: delight in the power of the human body, abandonment in the face of life having its way as only life can in pregnancy and birth. This baby was coming; life was on its way.

Baptism is about birthing. OK, this isn't really going to be a conversation starter at the dinner table either (although I'm starting to wonder why you're so eager to talk about baptism at dinner parties).

When we talk about baptism being an embodied theology, the birthing metaphor brings this embodiment into clear view. The waters of baptism are the birthing waters. They are the waters that nourish new life into being. In the previous section we spoke of seeing the waters of baptism as tomb. Now we are invited to see the waters of baptism as womb.

> Nicodemus came to Jesus by night and said to him, "Rabbi, we know that you are a teacher who has come from God; for no one can do these signs that you do apart from the presence of God." Jesus answered him, "Very truly, I tell you, no one can see the kingdom of God without being born from above." Nicodemus said to him, "How can anyone be born after having grown old? Can one enter a second time into the mother's womb and be born?" Jesus answered, "Very truly, I tell you, no one can enter the kingdom of God without being born of water and Spirit. What

is born of the flesh is flesh, and what is born of the Spirit is
spirit. Do not be astonished that I said to you, 'You must
be born from above.' The wind blows where it chooses,
and you hear the sound of it, but you do not know where
it comes from or where it goes. So it is with everyone who
is born of the Spirit" (John 3:2-8).

As he often does throughout the Gospel of John, Jesus is
speaking in a deeply symbolic sense in the above passage.
Being born from above can also be translated born anew
(or born again, as we so often hear). Jesus is speaking of a
spiritual rebirth, but he is using the earthy image of human
birthing. Nicodemus moves in a literal direction, thinking of
wombs and perceiving only impossibility.

You may think, after grappling with the difficult imagery
of baptism as dying, that now we are in the purely celebratory and joyful metaphor of baptism as birthing. But birthing
is itself a life *and* death situation. New life is determined to
come, yes. But it isn't guaranteed. And there are any number
of ways that the lives of both mother and infant are at risk
in the birthing event. Birth is also messy. It can be unpredictable. It's not a pretty thing.

Sometimes baptisms are a little messy and unpredictable
as well. Marcus Pomeroy is a spiritual director and retired
American Baptist pastor who served in churches for over
forty years. He remembers with some chagrin the first time
he baptized someone. "A deacon strapped me up," he explains. "Literally strapped me up. Strapped my wrists with
these things they use to seal out the water from getting onto
my shirt. And he buckled them pretty tight. By the time I
got into the baptistery, my hands had started swelling up,
because the straps were cutting off my circulation. When the
first candidate came down, my hands were about the size of a
catcher's mitt. It was awful.

"This first candidate had some challenges, and one of
them was a fear of water itself. And, along with that, a fear
of baptism. So when I started to baptize her, she let her feet
come up and she started floating. And then thrashing around

a bit. And she came up over the baptistery ledge, and all the congregation could see was her hand coming up and grabbing onto the shelf at the edge of the baptistery.

"I'm trying to baptize her, and she wouldn't close her eyes. So I'm looking right into her eyes, and I'm thinking, 'This is going so badly. This is awful.' My hands were totally numb by that time," Marcus laughs as he recalls. "It was just a really awful experience. None of the real transcendent stuff was happening at all. I remember thinking, 'I'm in over my head with this. I don't know what I'm doing here.' She didn't either, of course."

My son was baptized when he was eight years old. Doug and I had long conversations with him about his decision, and we felt he was ready despite his young age. But he was also afraid. He didn't know how to swim, and he was afraid of going under the water. When I shared his fear with my students at the time, they suggested we give him swimming lessons as his baptism gift. It was a marvelous idea, and it's exactly what we did. But the baptism happened before the swimming lessons started, so Elliot had to wade into the water in trust.

Because he was so small, the pastor decided to sink a small crate into the baptistery for Elliot to stand on. Unfortunately, that put him up a little too high, so he did not have the support of the water as the pastor began to dip him backwards. As he felt himself falling back, Elliot panicked briefly. His feet came up off the crate and kicked noisily as his head went under water. He came back up with a frightened expression that soon disappeared as he realized the worst was over.

My heart was broken for him, though. I had wanted his baptism to be transcendent, but it was messy. I wanted it to be safe, but it was frightening. I wanted it to be picture perfect, but it was honestly a little cringe-worthy.

My friend Sharon Fennema, who had come to witness Elliot's baptism, turned the experience around for me, though. She wrote me a letter after the event to say how meaningful it was to her to witness Elliot's kicking in the water. She experienced it as a visceral connection to power of life. That kick, that splashing of water, was Life Itself coming into being. When I shared this experience with Marcus, he suddenly could see his own experience differently.

"Gosh, that's so true," he said. "Birth itself is not pretty. It's a struggle. And it's a life-and-death struggle. So as a symbol of new life, baptism that is too smooth and pretty isn't a reflection of what's actually going on."

This realization brought another story to mind for him immediately. "I remember in El Salvador where we were at Terra Blanca Church. The priest was baptizing children. And he said, I'll never forget this: 'Parents, think about this. Think about what you're doing. Realize the risk that you are taking here. What you are inviting. What you are placing your children into: a life of radical love and selflessness.' And particularly in El Salvador," Marcus commented, "this meant a life that would be a challenge to the principalities and powers that were there."

One more story about birth. Sometimes I joke that the reason I have only one child is because six weeks after Elliot was born, I wrote down everything I could remember about his birth. I think maybe there's a reason we are supposed to forget, but I wrote it all down! Elliot was born at Bryn Mawr Birth Center outside Philadelphia. It was natural childbirth with no medication, and it was just the way I wanted it to be.

It was in the experience of giving birth that I came to know, vividly and unforgettably, the power that resides in pain. In the weeks leading up to my due date, the midwife coached my birthing class to understand that Western culture teaches us to react to pain by resisting it. We are taught to *fight* pain, to *defeat* pain, to *defy* pain, and to *numb* pain. But labor pains are different, she said. You should not resist labor pains, but *enter into them*. To fight pain, we tense our muscles. But to work with pain, we must relax into it. One way to know if you are fighting pain, she advised us, is to notice if you are clenching your teeth or not. If your teeth are clenched, you are fighting the pain. You have to relax your jaws instead, and keep your teeth apart.

The pain of labor, in my experience, creates its own space and its own time. But it is also a space and time that is utterly aware of *this* space and time. The contractions, as they grow in force and power, become absolute. They are all. *Everything.* There is nothing else but the contraction, the sound of the labor groans, the entering into the pain, the heart of the pain, the easing of the pain, and the momentary, blissful absence of pain.

The pain of labor is different from other pain, because it is meaningful from the start. The woman knows why she is in pain. It is a hopeful pain, though by no means danger-free—the hoped-for outcome is life, though the risk of death is ever-present.

But the force embodied in that pain is nothing less than the force of life. The pain of all life is distilled in those contractions. The birthing woman must find a way to work with that power, not to resist it; indeed, to *become* pain-and-power itself in order to bring forth life.

"We know that the whole creation has been groaning in labor pains until now; and not only the creation, but we ourselves, who have the first fruits of the Spirit, groan inwardly while we wait for adoption, the redemption of our bodies" (Romans 8:22-23). The early Christian mystic Paul wrote this to the Christian believers in Rome. All of creation groans with the resonant groans of labor. We are all caught up in those labor pains, those contractions of a cosmos longing to birth forth loving relationship and reconciliation. The groans ride on the power of the birthing cosmos. It is a pain that is absolute. It is everything.

The waters of baptism are meant to conjure this pain and the power in it. They are meant to evoke in us a deep body memory of the power of life and its will to exist. Marcus feels he encountered that power and life in his baptism even as a child. So much so that the memory of it comes back to him in times of struggle and heartache. "The times I remember I am baptized, then I remember I am connected to that energy. I have experienced that love-that-is-for-us, even Life itself. It is part of what it means for me to be me. I kind of get a bit tongue-tied as I try to say too much about it."

If we set up the expectation that baptisms are pretty or even quaint, then we miss out on the richness of what a messy baptism can mean to us later. To put it another way, when we understand that baptism is birthing in all its pain and power, then in our most painful moments the memory of our baptism becomes a gift of resiliency.

NOTES

1. Charles Joyner, *Down by the Riverside: A South Carolina Slave Community* (Urbana, IL: University of Illinois Press, 1984), xiii.

2. See World Council of Churches Commission on Faith and Order, *One Lord, One Baptism* (London: SCM Press, 1960), 53. Elizabeth Newman also investigates these connections in her chapter "Baptism: The Substance and the Sign." The emphasis for both the Commission and Newman is Matthew's construction of Jesus as Isaiah's suffering servant, particularly through his solidarity with sinful humanity. What stands out for me as I hold these two texts together is that both texts express God's uncontainable delight. See *Gathering Together: Baptists at Work in Worship*, ed. Rodney Wallace Kennedy and Derek C. Hatch (Eugene, OR: Pickwick Publications, 2013), 112.

3. This is Paul speaking again, by the way. He assures us of these things in Romans 8:38-39. Even so, I have to admit I'm still afraid of spiders.

CHAPTER **4**

BAPTISM AS BELONGING, FLOODING, BATHING, AND BECOMING

> to be called beloved
> is to ask the question
> what would it mean
> what would it look like if we actually believed
> that we are washed in God's grace
> —Emilie Townes[1]

BELONGING

THERE IS A funny thing about believer's baptism. In some ways it seems like it is all about the individual; it is representative of one person's decision to follow Jesus and to make that decision public through the act of baptism. In some congregations, a service of baptism will include the testimony of how an individual came to faith, what his journey was, what led her to these baptismal waters. We pray for the person who is being baptized. We light a candle that represents her faith. We celebrate his transformation.

And yet, baptism is not only about the individual. It is about a community that is being formed and reformed through this very act of baptism. Baptism is about belonging.

For Khalia Jelks Williams, a womanist theologian, ordained minister, and assistant dean of worship and music at Candler School of Theology in Atlanta, GA, baptism is first

35

and foremost an act of creating community. "We can't do this alone," she urges. "You can't do life alone. You can't try to figure out what it means to be a follower of Christ all by yourself. This can't be done in a vacuum. So the whole idea is that now you have entered into community." In a miraculous sense, not only does baptism provide the individual with a sense of deeply belonging to community, but the community is itself brought into being through the act of baptism. With each baptism that is celebrated, the community itself is born anew.

I asked each of the folks I interviewed where they saw God acting in baptism. For Khalia, the answer came quickly: "I see God at work in the community of people who have gathered at the baptism. Baptism becomes a point where God binds the community together," she explained.

In fact, when recalling her own baptism at age fourteen, she says, "Actually it's not the particular ritual itself that I remember, but the community around the ritual. When I think about remembering my baptism, it's really the people who were there that I remember. And it wasn't just my church. There was a group of churches that came together. Most of us who were baptized that evening were probably in our early teens. And I remember that it wasn't only our own local congregation but truly a network of congregations that formed together to receive us. And there was a big deal made of the fact that we were connecting, and that the whole community was making a commitment to each baptismal candidate. That continually resonates with me. It is so much more than journeying along this road by yourself. Baptism is the moment when the community says, 'We are journeying with you.'"

We need one another, that much is sure. Contrary to cultural messages that glorify individualism, it is our vulnerability in community that allows us to bind our wounds, minister to one another, and perceive the grace of God at work in the world. "No one person can fulfill all your needs," Henri Nouwen wrote in his book *The Inner Voice of Love: A Journey through Anguish to Freedom*. "But the community can truly hold you. The community can let you experience the fact that, beyond your anguish, there are human hands that hold you and show you God's faithful love."[2] The community holds us up at times, just as the water does when we let go and breathe.

Mylinda Baits finds both support and challenge in this: "The communal aspect of baptism informs what I'm about now, informs my ministry. It's a both/and kind of thing. It's a daily, personal recommitment to obedience and following, but also a daily recommitment to community care—to a sense of purpose beyond myself that propels me to care for others."

When visiting churches in her region in her role as executive minister, Marie Onwubuariri witnessed the baptism of a young man at Immanuel Baptist Church of Brookfield, Wisconsin. "Before the baptism, the community was invited to come forward to touch the water as a way to physically participate in the baptism, and also to recall their own baptism. It was very powerful. And it was effective in having me not only remember my own baptism, but to feel like I was a part of this young man's journey. I had an accountability to that even though I had never met him, and it was the first time I'd ever seen him. There was a litany in which we were called to be a part of this man's family, and I felt I was truly being called to be accountable to that."

The one being baptized is brought into a deeper sense of belonging. But as we can see in Mylinda's and Marie's experiences, at the same time, and perhaps even more importantly, the community is also being held accountable to a deeper belonging to the newly baptized and to one another. "So then you are no longer strangers and aliens, but you are citizens with the saints and also members of the household of God, built upon the foundation of the apostles and prophets, with Christ Jesus himself as the cornerstone. In him the whole structure is joined together and grows into a holy temple in the Lord; in whom you also are built together spiritually into a dwelling place for God" (Ephesians 2:19-22).

Baptism reminds us that we are all immigrants to Christianity, all former aliens of the faith. That means we come into community on equal footing with one another, as adopted beloveds, former strangers and wanderers, who are now members of God's very own household.

While baptism happens always on a local level—in a particular baptistery, pool, lake, or ocean—it is not only a local event but also a cosmic one. Every local baptism connects to every other baptism across place and time. Though we may fill the baptistery anew every time, the waters are always the same. The baptistery at Second Baptist Church in Germantown, Philadelphia, is filled with the same waters as Allen Temple Baptist Church in Oakland, which are the same waters that fill Sumi Baptist Church in Dimapur, India, which are the same waters that ran in the Jordan River when John the Baptist welcomed Jesus. We all pass through the same water and belong to a cosmic community of saints who rejoice at our passage.

Khalia notes that this cosmic relationship to the broader community has special meaning for Christians who feel connected to African ancestral roots. She remarks on the explicit connection that many African American Christians make between baptism and the African ritual of libations: "There is an ancestral connection with water that becomes present in baptism. We are joining *this* community, but we are also joining our ancestors who have laid the foundation of faith in this country. We are joining those who have shown us what it really looks like to be a Black Christian in the United States of America. We honor our ancestors *and join them* when we enter the water of baptism."

FLOODING

Many of us will not soon forget the terrible flooding of New Orleans in the days following Hurricane Katrina in 2005. We remember seeing people stranded on their rooftops, some of them with giant spray-painted signs that said, "Save us!" "Need Help!" and "Need Water." Hurricane Katrina is responsible for about 1500 deaths.[3] A former student of mine, Nataushia Miller, wrote movingly about her traumatic experience as a college student living through these terrible days in

New Orleans. Nataushia was evacuated soon after the storm hit and relocated to temporary housing at Centenary College in Shreveport, Louisiana. She was overwhelmed by feelings of grief, anger, and powerlessness as she watched loved ones fight to survive in the days following the storm. "No food, no clean drinking water, and no electricity, just waiting, waiting, and waiting—one day at a time." She remembers the stories of friends "sleeping in the hot humid heat of about 100 degrees, and lying next to dead bodies of men, women, children, and even babies. They felt like hostages and criminals because of the troops surrounding them with guns."[4]

Another of the world's worst natural disasters occurred less than a year earlier, on December 26, 2004, with the Indian Ocean tsunami. The severity of the storm was summarized ten years later in a report that noted: "A quarter of a million people lost their lives, five million required immediate aid and 1.8 million citizens were rendered homeless. The natural disaster, which caused extreme devastation over huge areas and the accompanying grief and anxiety, especially in Indonesia, Thailand and Sri Lanka, exceeded the imaginable and reached such drastic dimensions, mainly due to the lack of warning facility and a disaster management plan for the entire Indian Ocean region at this time."[5]

Our associations with water are sometimes traumatic, sometimes frightening, and sometimes painful. "I remember getting caught in a rip current down in North Carolina when our sons were small," Marcus Pomeroy told me. "I remember the feeling of utter helplessness when we noticed we were being washed out, away from shore. The boys were young. It was clear the current was strong enough that we couldn't swim against it. But just that morning we had attended a ranger talk about rip currents, and what to do if we encountered one. The boys were too far from me to get to them, but I was able to shout to them to swim parallel to the shore. And so we did. And we were able to get out of the rip current." Marcus paused for a moment as the memory continued to work in him. "Then we felt the power of the tide actually bringing us back to shore. So that was actually a pretty cool thing. And that became for me a sort of metaphor for the power of water that needs to be respected in our baptism as well."

The Lutheran liturgical theologian Gordon Lathrop writes: "Water is a source of life for us, and it figures large in our imagination of full life. . . . But water is not tame. Never far from our imaginations is the sense that, rising, it could drown us, wash away our place, destroy the signs of our centered cities. . . . Our very need for water means that in its symbolic sense, death is never far away."[6]

God's Spirit is not a tame thing. When we encounter it, sometimes we are filled with a sense of awe and even holy terror. (This feeling is what the poet of the Psalms would call the fear of God.) God's power is awesome, and even overwhelming at times. But God's promise to us is that we will not be harmed by God's power, only loved. "When you pass through the waters, I will be with you; and through the rivers they shall not overwhelm you; when you walk through fire you shall not be burned, and the flame shall not consume you . . . because you are precious in my sight, and honored, and I love you" (Isaiah 43:2, 4a).

When we pass through the baptismal waters, we take a step of faith; indeed, one in a series of steps, which says we trust God not to harm us but to love us. We give ourselves to this power that feels like it might be more than we could bear, but this power promises it will not consume us. And we don't just stick a toe in that water, but we bring our whole entire complicated selves into it.

More, we don't take control of our own baptism by simply bending our knees and immersing ourselves; rather, we give that power over to someone else. We let our bodies go slack as someone leans us backward, vulnerable as ever, and submerges us in water above our heads. Water that kills, but promises not to.

BATHING

In the film *The Lady in the Van*, actress Dame Maggie Smith brilliantly portrays Miss Mary Shepherd, a homeless woman who parks her van in the driveway of Alan Bennett for fifteen years in the 1970s and 1980s. Alan Bennett, the Oscar-nominated screenwriter of the film *The Madness of King George* (1995), wrote the script based on his experience with Miss Shepherd, allowing Smith to bring her vividly to life for us. She is difficult, abrupt, and deeply private. It's only with painstaking care that her story slowly unfolds for Bennett and for us, the viewers of the film. Though cantankerous, Miss Shepherd works her way into our hearts, and we come to love her despite what we suspect would be her vehement protest over any perceived sentimentality toward her.

When a social worker comes to take Miss Shepherd in for a brief visit to a care center for a bath and a meal, we can't help but feel Miss Shepherd's anxiety at the sudden invasion of her privacy, despite how gently and carefully she is handled. We see her dirty, worn face staring out over the steaming water of a gleaming, white porcelain bathtub. A nurse silently removes Miss Shepherd's scarf and walks over to lay it down on a nearby counter. She handles the scarf with care as if it's great value; although, we know it's just a rag at this point. And there are many layers of clothing yet to be removed. Miss Shepherd trembles with fear as her eyes fix on that steaming water in front of her.

We don't see any of the other layers removed, and we don't see the bath itself. But we do see Miss Shepherd walking down a hallway afterward, with her hair wrapped up in a towel and a warm bathrobe around her. The nurse holds her hand as they walk together. "You smell lovely," the nurse tells her.

Next, we watch as Miss Shepherd has her hair brushed and pulled back into a ponytail. You have the sense it's been decades since she's last been touched. Then, dressed, she enters a cafeteria and, not inconsequentially, sits at the table with a meal. (In worship, the bath always leads to the meal!) Miss Shepherd crosses herself (it's the only time we see her do this in the film). The cleansing bath, the welcome meal: she is remembering her baptism. And so do we.

Baptism is the bath we take in public. "Why do you delay?" Ananias implored Saul after his vision. "Get up, be baptized, and have your sins washed away, calling on his name" (Acts 22:16). Right there in the middle of worship, we enter the tub and find ourselves washed. "Not as a removal of dirt from the body," writes the author of 1 Peter, "but as an appeal to God for a good conscience through the resurrection of Jesus Christ" (1 Peter 3:21).

This is a most unusual bath, because in a sense it is one that is meant to cleanse us for all time. Sylvia Plath, who was well-acquainted with the depths of depression, wrote in *The Bell Jar*: "It seemed silly to wash one day when I would only have to wash again the next. It made me tired just to think of it. I wanted to do everything once and for all and be through with it."[7] In fact, that's what this public bath does for us. We enter the waters only once, and we are made clean ever after. Even so, life is still messy and difficult. We are still messy and difficult. And that's all right.

Mylinda was baptized when she was ten years old with her two older sisters. They'd been attending Sunday school and church with their aunt and uncle. "My uncle had come to faith at an AA meeting and was starting to feel more involved and connected at an American Baptist church. So that was our spiritual heritage," she told me.

"I remember it as being celebratory. There were lots of folks who were happy. My grandparents came, my parents came. And, as a result of that event, they became more curious about their own faith. And there was this whole sort of family system shift. So my parents came to faith, and were baptized. And my grandparents as well. And then my whole family started attending.

"My family had particular patterns of living that were non-Christian patterns. So that was sort of both a blessing and a burden. It was a way that I could see the church community struggling with the reality that change or transformation was taking a little bit of time. It wasn't an instant shift from the smoking, cussing, drinking patterns that were a part of our family system." Mylinda laughs as she recollects her early experience, though you can see some pain in her eyes as well. "Jesus didn't stop those things instantaneously. There was some pain of judgment in the community as well. But there was also grace. It was a mixed bag. We were, as I say, loved into the kingdom. And there were some wonderful, beautiful, grace-loving saints that loved us in spite of our dysfunctional functioning. And they invested specifically into my life, and made a big shift for me as to how I went about life. Yeah, it was the beginning of a change."

"You smell lovely," we might hear God say as God walks beside us through life. It may be a prophetic statement for us—an already-and-not-yet promise that, even if we stink to high heaven at the moment, our bath has transformed us nonetheless.

BECOMING

"Baptism offends our sense of self-sufficiency and demands we recalibrate life on God's terms," writes the British Baptist Andy Hickford. "Baptism is a rumour of another world, which confronts our own."[8] When we enter the waters of baptism, we change our citizenship status. The public act of baptism declares to the world that we have become citizens of God's kingdom and not Caesar's empire. John the Baptizer could not have been more explicit about this as he invited, or rather, implored his followers to repent and enter the waters of the Jordan. Bless the brave souls who were courageous enough to ask John to say more about his rough and fiery preaching. "What should we do?" they asked. John tells them: "'Whoever has two coats must share with anyone who has none; and whoever has food must do likewise.' Even tax collectors came to be baptized, and they asked him, 'Teacher, what should we do?' He said to them, 'Collect no more than the amount prescribed for you.' Soldiers also asked him, 'And we, what should we do?' He said to them, 'Do not extort money from anyone by threats or false accusations, and be satisfied with your wages'" (Luke 3:10-14). If we think John's baptism is radical, do we really expect that Jesus' baptism is any less so? If John himself says he was baptizing only in water, but that Jesus would baptize with Spirit and fire, then I strongly suspect the radical demands of baptism are only ratcheted up.

The experience of baptism calls us to a life of radical discipleship. It is what Khalia Jelks Williams calls "the baptismal life." She reflects: "What does it mean to live a baptismal life that says I am going to die to myself, my own selfish desires, my own ambitions, my own motivations, and I am going to come up, rise, live a life following Christ? What does a life of Christ exemplify? It's all about justice. All about subverting systems. All about love. All about compassion. And if that's the case, then living a baptismal life means committing to a life that says *in every area we are going to seek out justice, compassion, love, and mercy.* In the political spectrum, it becomes a requirement. To be professed as a *Baptist*, which says

BAPTISM AS CONQUEST AND RESISTANCE

The connection between baptism and politics is not a new, trendy idea. In fact, the connection between the two has a deep and sometimes painful history. The history of missionary movements includes churches' entanglement with imperial conquest; conversion and baptism (and sometimes *forced* baptism) were sometimes imposed on indigenous peoples around the world as a means of subduing them and bringing them under imperialist rule. For example, empowered by an edict of Pope Nicholas V in 1452, colonizers, slavers, and missionaries traveled together to the continent of Africa to kill, enslave, or forcibly catechize non-Christians to expand the Portuguese empire, the slave trade, and Christianity simultaneously.[1]

At the same time, baptism has also been a means of resistance to colonizing powers. For Sarah Bartmann, a Khoekhoe woman taken from her home and forcibly exhibited by an Englishman, Hendrik Cezar, baptism was "a claim to racial equality and an assertion of humanity."[2] The realization that baptism had the power to convey equality and humanity on converts was the reason white and European Christians sought to withhold evangelization and baptism from Africans and African Americans. As Yvette Abrahams points out, baptism had real political consequences: "Khoi people were rarely admitted to baptism in southern Africa, since Christianity was widely identified with a white skin, and baptism posed legal problems, theoretically compelling judges to give equal weight to Khoi and white testimony in court, and removing an informal bar to Khoi land ownership."[3]

NOTES

1. See Keith Augustus Burton, *The Blessing of Africa: The Bible and African Christianity* (Downers Grove, IL: InterVarsity Press, 2007), 197–198.

2. Yvette Abrahams, "Colonialism, Dysfunction and Disjuncture: Sarah Bartmann's Resistance (Remix)," in *Agenda: Empowering Women for Gender Equity*, no. 58, African Feminisms Three (2003): 21, http://www.jstor.org/stable/4548090.

3. Ibid., 21.

the entire foundation of who I am rests in this baptism that I've undergone, then I have to live out a *baptismal life* that focuses on matters of justice."

Just as John the Baptizer customized what that baptismal life looked like for his various followers, so Khalia sees diversity in how we engage our baptismal lives. "It looks different for each individual and each community. So you can't say, for instance, 'If you're not going out and protesting and marching, then you're not living a baptismal life.' There is no real rubric for it. But there do have to be events in the life of the congregation and the life of the individual that are about love, compassion, mercy, and justice. What are you doing in your local community? Are you ignoring people there? Does your ministry compel you to serve outside the walls in which you were baptized? And if it doesn't, then I do think you are missing that idea of living a baptismal life. There is an imperative connection there."

Marcus Pomeroy finds the "rubric" for baptismal life in Matthew's Gospel. "You know, at its most authentic, baptism is a recognition that I am taking a step to walk the path of Jesus, along with everything that means. I think within the church we have unfortunately sanitized that path too much. We are baptized, which means taking a step into a life where we are committed to feeding the hungry, visiting the sick, proclaiming liberty to the captives, and sight to the blind. It's essentially taking all of that on and trying to live that as radically and with as much integrity as possible. It is a radical step."

Baptist theologian Barry Harvey doesn't sugarcoat any of this. "Baptism is the sign and seal of a person's induction into a new *polis*, marking the passage from death to life and the transfer of rulership and change of allegiance from the powers of this world to the reign of God. . . . Immersion in the baptismal waters divests us of all previous definitions of identity based on class, ethnic or national origin, gender and family ties. It quite literally strips off the old human being with its practices, and clothes the one baptized with Christ's new humanity."[9]

If we knew all this, we might never be baptized. But what we must understand is that all of these imperatives, all of these demands of radical discipleship and faithful baptismal living, are made as an invitation to us to step into a life that is drenched in grace. We are empowered to do these things because we have encountered God's love for us and God's love for God's heartbreaking world. In our baptism, we express our desire to participate in God's liberating and loving action in the world. Do you see the distinction? We are not saying we will save the world—we would implode under such pressure as that. We are saying, though, that we desire to participate in God's saving of the world. "In my baptism, I am making a public proclamation that I am going to continuously deny self and continuously follow Christ," Khalia tells me. "I am literally saying I cannot do that on my own. I am relying on the Spirit's action, which is what brought me to my conversion and my baptism to begin with. I am relying on the Spirit to continue to empower me."

NOTES

1. Emilie Townes, "To Be Called Beloved: Womanist Ontology in PostModern Refraction," *The Annual Society of Christian Ethics* 13 (1993): 93.

2. Henri J. M. Nouwen, *The Inner Voice of Love: A Journey through Anguish to Freedom* (New York: Doubleday, 1996), 7.

3. John L. Beven, et al. "Annual Summary: Atlantic Hurricane Season of 2005," *Monthly Weather Review*, American Meteorological Society, 136:3 (March 2008): 1110. http://www.aoml.noaa.gov/general/lib/lib1/nhclib/mwreviews/2005.pdf.

4. Nataushia Miller, *Is Freedom Your Reflection in the Mirror?: 8 Steps to Overcoming Trauma* (Nataushia Miller, 2015), 34.

5. Helmholts Centre Potsdam—GFZ German Research Centre for Geosciences. "The tsunami-early warning system for the Indian ocean: Ten years after." Science-Daily. www.sciencedaily.com/releases/2014/12/141218120727.htm.

6. Gordon W. Lathrop, *Holy Things: A Liturgical Theology* (Minneapolis: Fortress Press, 1993), 94.

7. Sylvia Plath, *The Bell Jar* (New York: Harper Perennial, 2013), 128. Kathleen Norris reflects on this passage in her book *The Quotidian Mysteries: Laundry, Liturgy, and 'Women's Work'* (Mahwah, NJ: Paulist Press, 1998), 39–40.

8. Andy Hickford, *Making Waves: A Survivor's Guide to a Baptism Service* (Worthing, UK: Verité CM Ltd, 2009), 17.

9. Barry Harvey, "Re-Membering the Body: Baptism, Eucharist and the Politics of Disestablishment" in *Baptist Sacramentalism*, ed. Anthony R. Cross and Philip E. Thompson, vol. 5, Studies in Baptist History and Thought (Waynesboro, GA: Paternoster Press, 2003), 112.

CHAPTER 5

NAVIGATING THE WATERS
Questions of Practice in Baptism

> Baptism is the moment when the community says,
> "We are journeying with you."
> —Khalia Jelks Williams[1]

BAPTISM AS A PROCESS, NOT A MOMENT

When you ask people to tell you about their own baptisms, chances are each person will tell you about the moment he or she was baptized. People may describe the baptismal pool, the temperature of the water, the experience of going under the water and coming back up. We tend to think of baptism as an event—a singular moment that occurs on a certain day in our lives. Rarely, if ever, do we think of baptism as a process. And yet, baptism really is just that.

For many Baptists, the process is understood as beginning with a decision to follow Jesus; although, truth be told, we can back the process up a bit more and see that it begins with the sense of an invitation. It may be an invitation extended to us by a pastor, a Sunday school teacher, a parent, or a friend. The invitation may have been explicit: Have you considered making a decision for Christ? Have you thought about baptism? Or it may have been much subtler than that—a stirring in the spirit, a sense that what has been has not been enough, a longing for deeper connection with the Holy, a growing intimacy with God, a hunger, a thirst, a searching. And, of course, ultimately, the invitation comes from God: "You did not choose me," declares Jesus in the Gospel of John, "but I chose you" (15:16).

The process of my own baptism began in the quiet of my bedroom when I was about eleven years old. For several months, I had been reading my Good News Bible with its nifty denim cover. I had marked up its nearly see-through pages with bright yellow highlighter pens, and written my questions in the margins in big, looping letters. On this particular evening, I had a strong sense of God's presence with me. It was a gentle, grace-filled presence that felt full of welcome, kindness, and invitation. I felt my spirit quiet within me, and I found I wanted to do more in response to this warm presence. I bowed my head as I sat at my desk and began to speak to God. "I promise to give you my life," I told God. "Whatever you ask of me, I will do it. I promise."

It was not a prayer I'd heard anyone tell me to pray. It simply arose spontaneously from within me. I remember how closely the feeling of fear traveled on the heels of that promise. What *would* God ask of me? I wondered. What if it feels like more than I can do? "Regardless," my spirit responded in prayer to God. "Even if I am afraid. Even if I don't want to do it. I promise in this moment that I will do whatever you ask of me." This was when my baptism began.

The actual event of my baptism followed months later. The pastor of our church baptized my brother and me on the same Sunday. We were attending a United Methodist Church at the time, although our family had previously been part of an American Baptist congregation, where both Jef and I had been dedicated. I think our Methodist pastor was a bit scandalized when he realized, only a few weeks prior to my brother's scheduled confirmation, that Jef and I had never been baptized! (As longtime Baptists, it had never occurred to our family that we would undergo baptism before we had made our decisions to become followers of Jesus.) I don't remember taking part in any pre-baptism classes, just a one-time visit from the pastor with our family so he could establish that we were ready to take this next step. Even at the time, I remember feeling we were being baptized for the sake of expediency. Yet the event itself was still deeply meaningful for me. I remember the experience vividly, feeling in that moment of baptism the same loving, gentle, and invitational presence of God that I had felt in my bedroom the night I promised my life to God.

I think our churches could be much more intentional in thinking about baptism as a process that begins well before the event itself. While some churches may extend an invitation once or twice a year to young people to join in pre-baptismal classes, what if we deepened this experience by asking baptized members of the congregation to share a three-minute testimony of when they began to sense God's invitation to baptism in their own lives? These testimonies could be offered every Sunday during the season of Lent, a time traditionally set aside for preparation of baptism in early churches. If this practice were done annually, how might it allow people to listen more deeply to God's invitations in their lives at other times? Hearing a variety of stories may help people perceive the many ways God moves in people's lives. It would be wonderful to hear from people with powerful stories, but also people with very simple, almost ordinary stories. (So often we privilege the stories of radical transformation that those with less dramatic stories feel inferior or may miss entirely the still, small voice that leads to a loving relationship with God.)

In a similar way, I think we are often limited by thinking of baptism as an experience that ends the moment we emerge from the waters. I encourage churches to extend the experience of baptism with great intentionality. In the weeks following a baptism, name the newly baptized in your congregation's prayers, asking for God's continuing work in their lives, and for their continuing openness to God's work. Have members of a congregational care committee send a card or letter to the newly baptized member, at least a week after their baptism. I would even encourage you to consider sending monthly cards for the first year. If those who were baptized took part in new members classes or pre-baptismal classes in the weeks leading up to their baptism, consider offering at least a few classes after baptism. Use these times to talk together about the experience of their baptism, about deepening commitments of discipleship, and to encourage the formation of spiritual disciplines. You could invite church members to be guest speakers to these classes, to share their own experiences of discipleship with newly baptized members. What do they struggle with? What sustains them for the long haul?

If a church encourages godparents or sponsors for baptismal candidates, it could provide guidance for the kinds of continuing support they can offer in the weeks and even years to come. Encourage sponsors to pray daily for the baptized member, to reach out regularly and check on how they are doing, to encourage regular attendance at worship, and to remember the anniversary of their baptism with a note, card, text, or email.

Treating baptism as a process can help inform a more holistic and grace-filled Christian spirituality that encourages followers as they seek to live out their commitments to discipleship. Strong preparation and strong follow-through not only can help individual believers come to deeper experiences of faith but also can draw the whole community together around their shared baptismal identity. By sharing testimonies, planning on regular contact and celebration of baptismal anniversaries, and connecting baptism to a whole life of faith, we can all better understand ourselves as drenched in grace for a life of discipleship.

ON INFANT BAPTISM

The ecumenical disagreement between Christian churches that practice believer's baptism and churches that practice infant baptism has dominated Baptist writings about the practice of baptism; there is no shortage of information for the curious reader who may wish to further explore this topic.

In this book so far, I have intentionally attempted to direct our attention away from the debate about baptizing infants to focus our reflections more thoroughly on theology. Nonetheless, because believer's baptism (or the rejection of infant baptism) has been a steadfast commitment for Baptists (and a barrier to ecumenical cooperation), it is important to address its historical context as well as its theological significance.[2]

Tracing our theological origins back through both the radical reformers and the separatists alike, the earliest Baptists looked toward the witness of Christian Scriptures to reform church practices of their own time. Bill Leonard contends that, based on their reading of New Testament accounts of baptism, earlier generations of Baptists "insisted that the New Testament knew only a believers' church. Baptism was to be given only to those who had repented and professed faith in Christ—an action impossible for infants."[3]

In addition, both radical reformers and separatists were deeply committed to disentangling the church from the state. Whereas "Luther continued to link infant baptism and citizenship, extending the medieval relationship between church and state," Baptists vehemently rejected the connection.[4] Baptists contended that baptism must not be linked to becoming a citizen of any particular nation; rather, it is to incorporate us into the Body of Christ, to make us citizens of God's reign alone.

Writing about this in a contemporary sense, Barry Harvey urges us to understand that baptism is more than "an 'inner experience' of an individual."[5] Baptism instead realigns our allegiance from any particular state, tribe, or affiliation to God's kingdom made known to us through Jesus' life, death, and resurrection. "Immersion in the baptismal waters divests us of all previous definitions of identity based on class, ethnic or national origin, gender and family ties."[6]

Retaining these radical notions of the significance of baptism, Baptists might be able to better articulate a theological justification for refraining from baptizing infants. A re-alignment of one's full identity takes careful consideration. Such disaffiliation with other traditional markers of identity ought to be one that comes with conscious choice, inasmuch as this is possible.

THE RELATIONSHIP BETWEEN INFANT DEDICATION AND BAPTISM

Churches that practice believers' baptism must consider questions of how it is that children are included in the life of the church. Because baptism has been the means by which people are incorporated into the Body of Christ (and therefore, into the membership of the church), unbaptized children are caught in a kind of in-between status. They are already a vital part of the community, but they are not yet professed followers of Jesus, so they are not yet fully members of the church. In this context, the dedication of infants serves several functions, then. It provides a way for a congregation to celebrate and fully welcome the presence of a new child in their midst; it provides an opportunity for parents to bring their child before the congregation for blessing; and it gives both the parents and the congregation an opportunity to pledge their ongoing support and nurture of the child until she or he can make a decision to follow Jesus. This section will briefly address both the biblical foundations for practicing the rite of dedication (or blessing) in worship as well as the historical development of the practice. It will conclude with several recommendations for things to consider when performing dedications.

Both Hebrew and Christian Scriptures are often cited in support of infant dedication. In Deuteronomy 6:7, the Israelites are urged to "recite [these words] to your children and talk about them when you are at home and when you are away, when you lie down, and when you rise." Similarly, Proverbs 22:6 urges: "Train children in the right way, and when old, they will not stray." We also remember Hannah who, after many years of being childless, dedicates her son Samuel to God (1 Samuel 1:21-28). Of course, we also see precedent for dedicating and blessing children in the Gospels when Mary and Joseph bring Jesus to the temple to present him before God and for Mary to perform her purification rite (Luke 2:22-24; see also Exodus 13:2 and Leviticus 12:8)[7] and when Jesus allows the people to bring their children to him to be blessed (Mark 10:14-16; Matthew 19:13-15; Luke 18:15-17).[8]

Although there is a convincing case to be made that infant dedication services emerged in the fourth century during a period of several decades when children were not being baptized in the early churches,[9] today's practice of infant dedication most likely became common with the rise of the Sunday school movement in the mid-nineteenth century.[10] During this time churches increasingly understood that they needed to take on some of the responsibility for nurturing young children into faith. Sunday school took on an evangelistic emphasis that both increased the practice of infant dedication and lowered the average age of children seeking baptism.[11]

Here are a few recommendations for churches regarding the practice of infant dedication:

Make Dedications Distinct from Baptisms

One of my former students who pastors a Baptist congregation mentioned to me that he regularly incorporated water into his infant dedications because he thought they were intended to serve as "mini baptism services" that would hold the child over until his or her real baptism. With the awareness that many of our church members may come from different worshiping traditions or no church experience at all, we need to make it very clear that infant dedications are *not* the same as baptism. It is perfectly appropriate to include a brief explanation about the purpose of dedication as part of the service. A pastor might tell the congregation that we bring our children forward to bless them, to welcome them as beloved children in our community, to pledge our ongoing support for them and their parents, and to provide the parents an opportunity to commit themselves to their children's spiritual well-being. Dedication services are an expression of the church's commitment to be a community where children can grow in wisdom and knowledge of Christian faith as they come to know God's story as their story.

Make Dedications Broadly Participatory

Infant dedications are communal events. Rather than holding a separate service of dedication for each baby's birth, you could highlight the communal aspect of dedications by holding infant dedications once or twice a year. (Of course, this depends on the birth rate in your congregation!) Involve older children in the service as well. Invite all the children forward to move to the front of the church when the family comes forward. Some churches incorporate the rite of dedication into the children's message, making it clear that the children are themselves welcoming another little one into their community. You can include child-appropriate responses in the blessings or pledges. This can also be a wonderful opportunity for the congregation (and even parents of older children) to rededicate themselves to the promises they have made previously to love and support the older children in the church. The members of the gathered congregation can link together with one another during the prayer of blessing by each one putting their hands on the shoulders of those near them until the whole congregation is connected in prayer.

Focus on God's Story

As you prepare your litany of dedication or blessing, make it clear that, like all things in worship, this moment is an opportunity for us to know God's story as one that gives shape to our lives. Infant dedication bears witness to what God has done, what God is doing, and what God will do.[12] The rite should make clear that we affirm that the new children in our community are a part of God's great story of creation, love, faithfulness, forgiveness, salvation, and hope. Dedication "places them into the context of the church [and] celebrates the fact that God works through the home and the church to accomplish God's will."[13]

Be Flexible and Provide Options

Families are complicated and messy. In some cases, all family members may not be supportive of an infant dedication service. Perhaps a child's grandparents may desire the dedication service, but parents may not feel the need for it or may not attend church at all. One parent may desire the service, but the other may not. Some families may think they need to "get the baby done," but will not see how dedication is related to long-term vows made by parents and congregation members alike. As in all situations in working with families, pastors need to be discerning and flexible. A rigid approach to infant dedications may end up alienating families from the congregation rather than providing new inroads into the life of faith that a congregation offers.

In some circumstances, the language that refers to the "blessing" of the child may be more helpful than the term *dedication*. Arthur Patzia recommends renaming the rite "A Celebration of Birth" or, in cases where more than one child is present, "The Dedication and Blessing of Children."[14] Markus Thane argues that infant blessing is more theologically and biblically sound than infant dedication anyway.[15] (It is important to note that in England the word *dedication* is understood as another word for *blessing*.[16]) Just as a benediction or blessing is offered "at the end of each service as a means to equip and remind the believer that he or she is not alone during the struggles and challenges of the week, but that God will be with him or her," so infant blessings ask "for God's accompaniment in the life of the child."[17]

A final, personal thought about dedication. Our son, Elliot, was eight months old when he was dedicated at Central Baptist Church in Wayne, Pennsylvania. We never expected at that time that we would ever live far from the Philadelphia area. Even five years later when we moved to Berkeley, California, so I could begin my doctoral studies, we still expected we would be returning home after no more than a few years. When we joined Shell Ridge Community Church in Walnut Creek, California, a little over two years after we had moved, we celebrated that we had found a new church home, but we also deeply grieved the more permanent loss of our previous church home. Our son was only seven years old, and not yet baptized. Doug and I were keenly aware that the two of us were becoming full members at our new church, but Elliot would still be caught in an in-between status. So in conversation with the pastor, we turned to the dedication service we had used for Elliot seven years earlier and a continent away. When Doug and I joined the church, we asked the pastors to weave into the litany for new members a section in which our new congregation affirmed the promises made at Elliot's dedication by our former congregation. This liturgical moment served as a connecting point for our family—from one congregation to another, one promise to another, one holy moment to another. Hearing those promises spoken again by our new community helped Elliot know he had found a loving home in this new church, that God's presence had followed us from coast to coast. It gave a sacred significance to his in-between status that eventually led him to his own decision to follow Jesus and enter the baptismal waters.

CHILDREN, BAPTISM, AND THE MINISTRY OF PRESENCE

As mentioned in the previous section, the rite of infant dedication arose at least in part to address the need to find a way to welcome young people into the community of the church even as we acknowledge that they are not yet fully members until they enter the baptismal waters themselves. The question inevitably comes up: at what age can someone make that decision? In some sense, it is a question that must be asked and answered by each new generation of the church; that is, we can't answer it for everyone and for all time. At certain points in our history, only adults were permitted to be baptized.[18] At other times, very young children were welcomed to the waters. Thomas Halbrooks writes about special services geared especially to children at revivals that would place "considerable pressure on children to make a profession of faith."[19]

The children responded, and at younger and younger ages. In the early nineteenth century some as young as six to eight were responding, and by the 1920s there were some as young as four and five. The numbers of these continued to increase to the extent that by the 1960s the normative ages for responding had dropped from Juniors (ages nine to twelve) to Primaries (ages six to eight). Where were Baptists to draw the line?[20]

As recently as 2014, *Christianity Today* published an article titled, "Baptizing the Dora Generation" in which the author cites a Pastors' Task Force report of the Southern Baptist Convention declaring that "the only consistently growing group in baptisms is age five and under" and noting that the "preschool age group saw a 96 percent increase from 1974 to 2010." As of 2011, the denomination's Annual Church Profile groups together all children under the age of eleven in their statistical reporting.[21]

On the other hand, several of the people I interviewed for this book recalled that, in the congregation of their youth, there was some expectation that young teens would participate in baptism preparation classes and undergo baptism.

Donald Ng, former president of American Baptist Churches, USA and retired pastor, remembers: "All my closest friends got baptized together. It was peer pressure. It was like, when one person said, 'I'll get baptized,' then everyone signed up." Although Don says he felt some pressure to join his friends, he did not choose to do so immediately:

> I became consciously aware that I wasn't ready, so I didn't go forward. I started to question my own faith. I started to ask questions about being raised a Baptist. I wondered why I wasn't able to go forward. And basically, eventually, it came down to a sense of a timetable. I realized I was getting older. And I thought, if I didn't baptized soon [laughs] I wouldn't get baptized until I was maybe out of high school! So I got baptized. But even after I was baptized, I still had

questions. So the pastor of the church invited me in, one-on-one, and I asked tough questions about what it really means to be baptized. So it was really the dialogue that I had with my pastor that led me to understand the meaning of baptism, and what it means to be a Christian disciple. I eventually brought this experience into my own ministry as a pastor where I take baptism very seriously. It's more than just a rite of passage. I often invoke Bonhoeffer and say that baptism reminds me there is a cost to discipleship.

In his book *Contemplative Youth Ministry*, Mark Yaconelli urges congregations to recognize the significance of being fully present with young people. "When youth are seen, they feel valued. When they are heard, they feel respected. When someone is moved by their situation, they feel loved. When they receive kindness, they feel cared for. And when others delight in their existence, they sense the very breath of God."[22] Yaconelli reminds us that it is never too soon to listen, love, and be fully present to the young people in our churches and communities. When we form genuine relationships with young people, then it will become clear when they are ready to enter the process of baptism.

Yaconelli believes that the goal of youth ministry is "to hold a young person's deepest identity until he or she is able to see it too."[23] Children are more than merely prospective members; more, even, than potential disciples or merely maturing participants.[24] Yaconelli confronts us with the questions: "How would we treat youth if we weren't trying to convince them of the importance of the faith, the worthiness of Jesus, the necessity of the church? What would happen if we sought to minister to young people through our ear, through our presence, through silent prayer and an open heart? What would such radical acceptance evoke in young people?"[25] A sensitive response takes into account each person.

Almeda M. Wright is a professor of religious education at Yale Divinity School. Her research focuses on African American religion, adolescent spiritual development, and the intersections of religion and public life. In her recent book

The Spiritual Lives of Young African Americans, she employs a method of "radical listening" to "African American youth for whom Christianity is still significant, but who are attempting to navigate Christianity, social media, and communal violence in a world where there is a naïve but growing expectation that racism and violence against youth of color is not (or should not be) prevalent anymore."[26] Through her process of listening deeply and radically, Wright concludes that one must eventually be able to "declare abundant life" such that "it proclaims *life as an option* in a world that loves death"; and "it embodies *limitless hope* in God, in one's self, and in the world."[27]

If our churches offer baptism in this context—a context of radical listening, of deep presence, with a complex understanding of abundant life, and a richly informed theological perspective on baptism—then we will be able to listen for when people (young and old) tell us they are ready to enter the waters. We might extend the invitation, but it is through the ministry of presence to the whole person that we will sense together when the time is right.

BAPTISM CLASSES: BEFORE *AND* AFTER

Liturgical historians have noted the common practice of enrolling new converts to Christianity into the catechumenate ("from the Greek verb *catecheo*, meaning 'to instruct' or 'to resound or echo in the ear'")[28] where they would be instructed about what it means to be a follower of Jesus. The nature of these classes, and how long the catechumenate lasted (anywhere from three weeks to three years) varied among different regions and across different centuries. Recently, catechesis has been reinvigorated, especially in more liturgical traditions as these churches increasingly work with adult converts to Christianity. Catechesis was focused primarily on spiritual formation, prayer, and learning the faith of the church.

What is striking about catechesis is that it did *not* focus on baptism itself. Reflection on baptism was saved until after the new converts had undergone their own baptisms. These after-baptism classes were called *mystagogy* and focused on "the meaning and life-long implications of what the reception of this baptismal gift entails."[29] The modern liturgical renewal movement has caused a resurgence of interest in mystagogy. In the Roman Catholic Church, it is common for adult converts to attend weekly classes throughout the season of Easter (the fifty days between Easter and Pentecost) and to attend monthly classes for a full year after baptism. Classes focus on the meaning of baptism, the celebration of the Eucharist (communion is received for the first time after baptism), and Christian living. In summary, liturgical historian Maxwell Johnson recommends that "the churches get busy on life-long mystagogy and the life-long return to the font as Christians seek to live out in the Spirit the implications of their new birth!"[30]

This is an area in which I think we who call ourselves *Baptist* might have much to learn from our sisters and brothers in other Christian traditions. "So often, once baptism happens, *that's it*," Don Ng lamented. "We really need to pay attention to post-baptismal care. I sought it out when I was a kid, and it made all the difference for me. But most people won't seek it out. And most churches don't offer it." How might it be for our newly baptized to continue to gather along with other long-term members of the church, at first weekly and then monthly, to discuss the meaning and significance of their baptismal experiences, to reflect deeply on the importance of receiving communion and being community, to engage in service work and ministry as an expression of their new baptismal identity? If the newly baptized had opportunities to talk regularly with those who have been baptized years (and even decades) ago, then their experience of their faith will mutually deepen.

Our common sharing about what our baptism means for us, and our story-telling about how we have experienced God moving in and for our lives could be understood in terms of that beautiful Baptist tradition of testimony. Informed by the work of Cheryl Townsend Gilkes, Almeda Wright lifts up testimony as one of the key "elements that will hold youth even as they critically engage and reflect upon their experiences in the world around them."[31] Addressing the role of testimony in the spiritual lives of young African Americans in particular, Wright remarks:

> I argue that it is essential to nurture youth in this practice, as the practice of sharing testimonies models for youth ways of sharing and addressing individual and communal concerns. I also found that practicing testimony sharing with youth serves to nurture youth in the legacy and narratives of African American communities and empowers youth to participate in transforming and renewing the traditions of African American communities.[32]

This was the experience of a former student of mine, Cherri Murphy. Cherri knows that she learned from "watching women, *particularly women*, testifying to their resiliency. They were testifying to what was happening in their lives in that moment. But at the end they always testified that it was going to change." The testimony of "faithful resiliency" and the "commitment to change" is what "put cement in my back," says Cherri. "That was what anointed me: this commitment not to the way things look at any given moment, but to the belief that our circumstances will change. So whenever something happens here locally or nationally, my mind goes back to those testimony services. I remember my ancestors, and their making it. And I know that in my moment, I shall make it, too."[33]

Learning to tell our stories in the overarching context of God's story, and learning to radically listen to one another as we tell these stories, builds our own sense of deep connection, resiliency, and well-being. I believe the practice of baptism itself provides an opportunity to engage more intentionally with one another in this practice of testimony and faithful storytelling in such a way that our lives, our churches, and our communities can be transformed into "cement-in-the-back" places of empowerment.

AFFIRMATION OF BAPTISM

It is quite possible that if we paid attention to post-baptismal care in the way I have just described then pastors might field fewer requests by church members to be rebaptized. In an early conversation with Marie Onwubuariri while this book was still in its formative stages, Marie admitted to me, "Um, so I read through your introduction, and there was a line in there that says baptism only happens once. And I chuckled at that." Born in the Philippines, Marie was baptized as an infant in the Roman Catholic Church. Marie's family immigrated to the United States when she was a toddler and they joined an American Baptist congregation. She continues:

> Typically in our church, those of us who grew up in the church got baptized between twelve and fourteen years old. I don't recall it as peer pressure, but I do recall it as routine. So I got baptized [for a second time] around that age. I have just faint memories of baptismal classes or new member classes or something. It isn't a bad memory or anything. But I just don't really remember much about it at all. And I don't remember anything happening post-baptism. I don't think I was very inquisitive as a kid, so I don't think I asked any questions about it.

As Marie grew from adolescence to young adulthood, she remained connected to her faith, but says she "wasn't actively engaged in thinking about myself as a Christian." However, after college, on occasion she would attend a Pentecostal church with a friend.

> That church had a practice of having an annual baptism at the beach in Long Island. And it wasn't just for new believers. Several members would get rebaptized, and a few even every year, and it was considered a recommitment, an annual time to check: Are we living out our faith? Are we being faithful to our call as disciples?

It was also at that time that I was experiencing a call to ministry. I had made a personal decision to reconnect with Christ, so I was already wanting to go deeper into faith. Worshiping with this other congregation helped me process that and think about things more.

So Marie responded to the invitation, and was baptized a third time. "I hesitate to talk about this in Baptist circles," she told me. "But it's really that third baptism that I go back to when I think about my call and my life. I don't know. I haven't really unpacked that so much. But for me, it was the third one that 'took.'"

Liturgical historian Paul Bradshaw has brilliantly pointed out that if we come across evidence that a particular liturgical practice was prohibited, we can be certain this is because people were already doing it. I wonder how many of us have stories like Marie's. I know I do.

I have shared already about my experience of being baptized when I was twelve. What I didn't mention is that this was my first baptism. I was baptized a second time in a lake at a Christian festival called Jesus '83. Although my baptism had been extremely significant to me, at this festival I encountered a preacher who was able to tap into that profound sense of anxiety that can sometimes reside at the center of our beings: Have I done enough? Am I *really* saved? Was my heart truly sincere? I responded to the preacher's call and joined the long line of people at the lakeside. I remember entering the water, wading toward the ministers stationed in the lake, and bending backwards as they lowered me beneath the water: my second baptism. Like Marie, at least until this moment, I haven't shared this experience widely!

What I think these stories tell us, though, is that many of us feel a need to revisit our baptisms. Whether we feel as though we have fallen away from God, or our commitment has grown deeper and more meaningful over time, or we find ourselves questioning whether we really were old enough when we made our initial decision to be baptized, or perhaps we grew up in a tradition where that decision was made on our behalf when we were infants—for these reasons and more, we may desire to return again to the baptismal waters. This is precisely why I believe a more robust theology of baptism can help us.

Although I'd been Baptist for many years, it wasn't until seminary when I was surrounded by Lutherans that I heard people talk about remembering their baptism. At first it seemed nonsensical to me: Why were Lutherans talking about "remembering" their baptism when they had all been baptized as infants? Truly, they had no "memory" of their baptism at all! And yet here they were at our daily chapel services at the Lutheran Theological Seminary at Philadelphia, touching the water in the font as they entered worship, and touching their wet fingers to their foreheads—remembering their baptism. Then, every Lent while I was in seminary, our professor of worship, Gordon Lathrop, would walk up and down the aisle with wet boughs taken from the pine tree just outside, shaking it vigorously so water sprinkled across the room, spraying droplets on our clothes, our hair, our foreheads, our glasses—remembering our baptism. And then there were the greeting cards that would arrive for my fellow students from their families and congregations every year—cards celebrating the anniversaries of their baptisms. It's true, my friends had no specific memory of their actual baptisms. But they remembered God's promises made to them in that moment; they remembered the gift of abundant grace; they remembered that they were woven into the fabric of God's story—and that they remained there, by God's grace, today.

As Baptists, we can do better at remembering our baptisms. We can do this by engaging in more theological conversations about baptism. Reading and studying this book together can be a great start! We can also remember our baptisms in our worship services. Like our more liturgically minded sisters and brothers, we can affirm our baptisms through litanies and prayers. These can show up organically during the season of Lent for those of us who follow the Christian year together.

Lent was initially set aside by the early church as a time of preparation for baptism. That is why the Revised Common Lectionary often includes readings that focus on water and baptism during this season. We could also remember and affirm our baptisms at Epiphany, when the biblical accounts of Jesus' baptism are highlighted.

Of course, the members of a congregation can join together in affirming their own baptisms whenever a new believer is baptized. We can do this by walking past the baptistery and touching the water—not because it holds any magical significance, but because we need these kinds of embodied, ritual moments to remind ourselves that God's grace is fluid and all-enveloping. Finally, as we will discover in the chapters to come, we can remember and reaffirm our baptisms whenever we approach the communion table, knowing with confidence that this is the place where we can be welcomed into God's gracious presence time after time, where we are formed into that blessed and beloved community that God so desires for us, where we can be sustained and nourished for the long journey of faith.

The truth is, there is no need for an individual to be baptized more than once. God's grace is not to be won, it is freely given—and it has no expiration date, either. If we have been welcomed into the baptismal waters once (whether as an adult believer or as an infant), there is no need for any of us to go through them again. What I am convinced we do need, however, is to remember our baptisms. In remembering our baptisms, we will live into the call of faithful discipleship from a place of grace.

NOTES

1. Khalia Jelks Williams, interview by author, Berkeley, CA, 2017.

2. A recent and increasingly common self-critique by Baptist theologians has been the lack of attention we have given to the theological meanings of baptism, especially given its apparent centrality to our identity. As the British Baptist Stephen R. Holmes sums it up: "Baptist writings on baptism rather rarely get beyond this polemical point concerning praxis, arguing far more about the mode (immersion) and subjects (believers only) of baptism than about the meaning and effect of the sacrament/ordinance. Perhaps bizarrely, Baptists have been remarkably poor at developing a theology of baptism over their history, often resting content with developing an

account of proper administration of the rite." See *Baptist Theology* (New York: T & T Clark International, 2012), 90.

3. Bill J. Leonard, *Baptist Ways: A History* (Valley Forge, PA: Judson Press, 2003), 19.

4. Leonard, 18, 19.

5. Barry Harvey, "Re-Membering the Body: Baptism, Eucharist and the Politics of Disestablishment," in *Baptist Sacramentalism*, ed. Anthony R. Cross and Philip E. Thompson, Vol. 5 (Waynesboro, GA: Paternoster Press, 2003), 112.

6. Harvey.

7. The Leviticus text provides the instructions for Mary's purification rite. Note that Mary needs to opt to bring the offering allowed for women who cannot afford a sheep.

8. For exegetical reflections on some of these texts, see Markus Thane, "A Theological and Liturgical Basis for the Baptist Practice of Child Dedication," *American Baptist Quarterly* 28 no. 2 (Summer 2009): 223–246. See also Arthur G. Patzia, "Baby Dedication in the Believers' Church," *American Baptist Quarterly* 3 no. 1 (March 1984): 63–72.

9. See David F. Wright, "Infant Dedication in the Early Church," in *Baptism, the New Testament and the Church: Historical and Contemporary Studies in Honour of R.E.O. White*. ed. Stanley E. Porter and Anthony R. Cross, Journal for the Study of the New Testament Series, Vol. 171 (Sheffield, England: Sheffield Academic Press, 1999), 352–378.

10. Patzia, 66.

11. Thomas Halbrooks, "Children and the Church: A Baptist Historical Perspective," *Review & Expositor* 80 no. 2 (Spring 1983): 182–183.

12. Patzia, 68–71.

13. Patzia, 71.

14. Patzia, 69.

15. Thane, 239–244.

16. See "Dedication" in *The New Westminster Dictionary of Liturgy & Worship*, ed. Paul Bradshaw (Louisville: Westminster John Knox Press, 2002), 154.

17. Thane, 241.

18. See Doug Adams, *Meeting House to Camp Meeting: Toward a History of American Free Church Worship from 1620 to 1835* (Saratoga, NY: Modern Liturgy Resource Publications, 1981), 62, and Thomas Halbrooks, "Children and the Church: A Baptist Historical Perspective," *Review & Expositor*, 80 no. 2 (Spring 1983): 181.

19. Halbrooks, 183.

20. Halbrooks, 183.

21. Kevin P. Emmert, "Baptizing the Dora Generation: Why Preschooler Faith is So Controversial," *Christianity Today*, June 10, 2014, https://www.christianitytoday.com/ct/2014/june-web-only/sbc-preschool-baptisms-under-age-6-southernbaptists.html. The cited task force report is no longer available.

22. Mark Yaconelli, *Contemplative Youth Ministry: Practicing the Presence of Jesus* (El Cajon, CA: Youth Specialities, 2006), 121.

23. Yaconelli, 121.

24. In an article written decades ago for the journal *Review & Expositor*, Thomas Halbrooks identified four basic approaches Baptists have taken toward children concerning their relationship to the church. He lists them in the order they occurred historically from the seventeenth through the late twentieth centuries. While limiting his study to specifically Southern Baptist contexts, I think many of us can see resonance in his categories with other Baptist settings. According to Halbrooks, children have been understood primarily as nonmembers, prospects, potential disciples, or maturing participants. See "Children and the Church: A Baptist Historical Perspective," *Review & Expositor* 80 no. 2 (Spring 1983): 179–188.

25. Yaconelli, 121–122.

26. Almeda M. Wright, *The Spiritual Lives of African American Youth* (New York: Oxford University Press, 2017), 5. For more about Almeda Wright's method of radical listening see Almeda M. Wright with Laura Everett and Bill Lamar, "Listening to Christian Youth," January 23, 2018, in episode 6 of *Can These Bones Live*, Faith & Leadership Duke Divinity School, podcast, MP3 audio, 48:53 https://www.faithand leadership.com/episode-6-almeda-m-wright-act-radical-listening-young-christians.

27. Wright, *Spiritual Lives*, 207. Emphasis is Wright's.

28. See "Catechumen, Catechumenate," in *The New Westminster Dictionary of Liturgy & Worship*, 98.

29. Maxwell E. Johnson, *The Rites of Christian Initiation: Their Evolution and Interpretation* (Collegeville, MN: The Liturgical Press, 1999), 240.

30. Johnson, *Christian Initiation*, 373.

31. Wright, *Spiritual Lives*, 218. Wright refers her readers to Cheryl Townsend Gilkes, *If It Wasn't for the Women* (Maryknoll, NY: Orbis, 2001), 127–138.

32. Wright, *Spiritual Lives*, 222–223.

33. I have written more extensively about Cherri Murphy and her community Second Acts in "Contemporary Liturgical Resources," in *Sources of Light: Resources for Baptist Churches Practicing Theology*, Perspective on Baptist Identity Series, ed. Steven R. Harmon and Amy L. Chilton (Macon, GA: Mercer University Press, 2019).

CHAPTER **6**

WORSHIP RESOURCES FOR SERVICES OF BAPTISM

I N THE FOLLOWING section you will find worship resources to help you celebrate baptisms, affirmations of baptisms, and infant dedications or blessings. Some of the resources will be complete liturgies. Others will be prayers or litanies that can be woven into existing services. Contributors to this section come from diverse contexts and help us to see the rich tapestry of faithful practices.

While these are newly crafted prayers and worship materials, keep in mind that repeating the same liturgy for each service of baptism, affirmation of baptism, or infant dedication can be deeply meaningful to a congregation. As people hear the same liturgy that has been used before, they are invited to remember previous baptisms—their own baptisms, their children's baptisms, and other baptisms that have happened in their churches. The same is true for communion services. Using the same services from year to year can help us make those cosmic connections across time and place.

However, incorporating new language in our worship services can help us facilitate more robust experiences. Using different prayers or litanies can draw out more clearly some of the rich theological themes that we have discussed earlier in this book. You might use the resources here in their entirety or let them serve as inspiration for writing your own liturgies.

WORSHIPFUL WRITING

If you would like to craft your own prayers, litanies, or services of dedication, baptism, and affirmation, you may find the following suggestions helpful.

Begin with Prayer

Whenever you write or plan anything for worship, let the planning experience itself be worshipful. Begin by opening yourself to the presence of God. Invite God to lead you in your writing process, so that the Spirit might pray in and through you. Do not rush through this time of prayer, but let your own spirit come to rest in the loving and gracious presence of God.

Bring Your Community with You into Your Prayer

As you continue to pray, bring to mind the baptismal candidates or the infants who will be dedicated, their families, and the congregation. Again, do not rush this moment, but slowly and intentionally let people's names and faces take shape for you. Invite God's blessing on them and pray that they might be open to the movement of the Holy Spirit through their experience in worship. Invite God to breathe life into this part of worship for the whole congregation that they might be renewed in their own baptismal commitments through their participation in this part of worship. You may find it helpful to go sit in the pews of the church, or to sit beside the baptistery when praying for the community at this point. Physically locating yourself in the places where the congregation sits or will experience the service can help you pray with even greater clarity.

Center Yourself in Scripture and Theological Themes

Slowly and prayerfully read Scripture texts that focus on dedication or baptism. Read the Scripture silently, but also read it aloud. It's common to notice different details or nuances in Scripture when we hear it spoken. Read through the passage in this way two or three times. As you do so, pay attention to the imagery in the Scripture. What pictures from the scene come to mind? Is there water? Dirt? Darkness? Are there stones? People standing around? Disciples? Is Jesus present in the scene? If so, where? What is the expression on his face? How is he holding his body? Try to imagine the scene as vividly as possible.

Pay attention, too, for any sounds in the scene. If there is water, what sound does it make? Can you hear people's footsteps on the ground? If there is darkness, is there also an oppressive silence? If there are voices speaking in the passage, what is their tone? Again, try to hear the text as vividly as you can. Seek to immerse yourself completely in the richness of the biblical text so that it might inspire—breathe life into— the litany, prayer, or liturgy you are about to write.

Ask God to help you know what the good news in this text is. Where is the hopeful word? The word of challenge and grace? If there is material in the text that resonates with the theological themes discussed in chapters 3 and 4 of this book, you may wish to reread those sections as well. Allow the images and metaphors to steep within you. Ask God to help you write a liturgy where the richness of Scripture and the good news of God's grace will shine forth through the congregation's participation.

Write the Liturgy

Using language and images that came to you in your time of prayer and reading, write your litany, prayer, or liturgy. Remember, less is often more. Use brief but evocative language to convey your ideas. You may find it helpful to keep the following structures in mind:

Baptism
+ Invitation for the Candidate(s) to come forward
+ Scripture Reading
+ Prayer
+ Affirmation of Faith / Baptismal Vows

+ Testimony from the Candidate(s)
+ Baptism
+ Community Response
  ⬩ May include words from sponsors or godparents
  ⬩ May include a Remembrance or Affirmation of Baptism
  ⬩ May include the Right Hand of Fellowship
+ Blessing
+ Lord's Supper

Infant Dedication
+ Invitation for the family (or families) to come forward (with sponsors)
+ Invitation for other children and youth to sit near the front
+ Scripture Reading
+ Brief Explanation of the Rite
+ Promises made by the parents, sponsors, children in the congregation, and congregation
+ Renewal of promises made to the children and youth of the church
+ Blessing of the Infant(s)

Read Aloud What You Have Written

Before publishing your liturgy in the bulletin or bringing it into the worship service, read aloud what you have written. Pay attention to how the words flow. Are there any clunky words that might cause you or the congregation to trip up a bit as you read them? If so, see if you can reword what you've written so that it will be easier to say. It is important to read it aloud because our tongues trip over things our minds may not.

End with Prayer

When you believe you've completed writing your liturgy, pray one more time with it. Ask God to bless its use so that the experience in worship may come alive for people and draw them into meaningful encounter with God's presence. Then, let go of what you have helped to create. It is not our responsibility to try and make the congregation feel any particular feeling in worship. We are only to gather for worship and allow God's Spirit to take it from there. We create our liturgies with as much care and attention as we can, and we hold them lightly after that. None of it is up to us to accomplish.

We Gather at the River [or Baptismal Pool]
Paul Schneider

Welcome and Introduction

Pastor: In the beginning of creation, the Spirit of God
moved over the waters, and with words, they were
transformed. Through all of Scripture, water remains
a primal force, capable of cleansing and renewing. At
the beginning of Jesus' ministry, he came to the river for
baptism. That river was just a river, that water was just
water, yet with the words of John the Baptist, a servant
of God the Creator, they were transformed. Baptism is
an ordinance, a command from our Savior, Jesus Christ,
to his disciples and all who follow. It has been done by
the church from its first days onward. Today we invite
[baptismal candidate's name(s) here] to join the great
flood of witnesses. This water is just water, this river,
just a river, but with the words we share today, it will be
transformed, as will our [brother(s) and/or sister(s)].

Prayer of Invocation

Pastor: Let us pray together: God, who brought forth all that is
from the waters of creation, be here today. Jesus Christ,
Lord and Savior, by your command, we bring these
fellow children of God to the waters to be cleansed and
transformed. Holy Spirit, our helper and inspirer, may
your presence make these waters and this moment a
flood of renewal. Amen.

What Scripture Has to Say

Reader 1:   The prophet Isaiah reminded us: "thus says the
Lord . . . Do not fear, for I have redeemed you; I have
called you by name, you are mine. When you pass
through the waters, I will be with you; and through the
rivers, they shall not overwhelm you." [Isaiah 43:1-2a]

Reader 2:   Jesus said: "Very truly I tell you, no one can enter the
kingdom of God without being born of water and
spirit." [John 3:5]

Reader 3:   Peter's call to those who first came to believe in Christ
after his resurrection was this: "Repent, and be baptized
every one of you in the name of Jesus Christ so that

your sins may be forgiven; and you will receive the gift of the Holy Spirit. For the promise is for you, for your children, and for all who are far away, everyone whom the Lord our God calls to him." [Acts 2:38-39]

Hymn or Musical Interlude

Prayer of Blessing the Waters

PASTOR: Holy God, you have given us water, and made it vital to our being. Just as we wither without your love, we are desiccated without these waters. Grant now that this water may be transformed, that it may become a renewing flood, a cleansing stream. May these waters be for [candidate] waters of a new birth. Lead them through these waters, as you lead your people through the sea, as you led your Son to the river, and as you have led so many witnesses of the Good News before today. You have already given us the Word in Jesus Christ; now send your Holy Spirit upon us, and these waters, that [candidate] may be forever transformed, and be one of your faithful children always. In the name of Christ Jesus, we pray. Amen.

Personal Affirmation

[*The pastor and baptismal candidate enter the waters.*]

PASTOR: Jesus commanded his disciples to go out to all the world, to make disciples of every nation. It is for this reason that we have come here today. The love of God has touched [candidate name].

Do you, [candidate name], believe in God, our Creator, Jesus Christ, our Savior, and the Holy Spirit, our great Helper?

[CANDIDATE]: I do.

PASTOR: Do you repent of your sins, which separate you from God, and do you allow the flood of Christ's grace to cleanse them from you, accepting the guidance of the Holy Spirit to turn you to a new path, following our Lord?

[CANDIDATE]: I do.

PASTOR: Do you accept Jesus Christ as your Lord and Savior?

[CANDIDATE]: I do.

Statement [or Testimony] of [Candidate]

The candidate may make here a brief statement or testimony.

Baptism

PASTOR: Having heard your witness, we now baptize you into the communion of the saints.

I baptize you in the name of God, Creator of the Heaven and the Earth.

[Submerge candidate, bring them up]

I baptize you in the name of Jesus Christ, our Lord and Savior.

[Submerge candidate, bring them up]

I baptize you in the name of the Holy Spirit, our constant Companion.

[Submerge candidate, bring them up]

Arise from the flood of new life, [*Candidate's full name (new name possible here)*] and know that you are now a member of the Holy catholic Church, the communion of all the saints, and the community of [*church name*].

Personal Response

PASTOR: Do you, [*Candidate*] promise to commit to a life of fellowship and worship with the church?

[CANDIDATE]: With God's help, I will.

PASTOR: Do you accept the gifts of God's love and grace, and will you accept the challenge and joy of following Jesus Christ?

[CANDIDATE]: With God's help, I will.

PASTOR: Will you strive to live out the Good News of God's love, as seen in Jesus Christ, in both word and deed?

[CANDIDATE]: With God's help, I will.

Community Response

PASTOR: In this moment, we all should remember our own baptisms. As we recall those waters, let us affirm to help [*Candidate*] in their walk with Jesus.

Do you, community of faith, representing the whole Church, promise to share with [*Candidate*] that which you yourselves have received: the gifts of God's love and grace, as revealed in Jesus Christ?

[COMMUNITY]: With God's help, we will.

[The pastor and candidate exit the water.]

Hymn or Musical Interlude

[The pastor and candidate can get dressed and/or dry off during this hymn.]

Blessing

PASTOR: We welcome you, Child of God. Your creator has brought you through the flood, transformed you in the waters. Come, and join your community, your family in Jesus Christ. May the love of God, the truth of Jesus Christ, and the blessings of the Holy Spirit be with us all. Amen.

Litany for the Newly Baptized,
the Community of Believers, and the Minister

(Prepared in Light of the Naga Baptist Christian Context for Baptism Worship Service)

SASHINUNGLA PONGEN

(The pastor or the worship leader may kindly invite the newly baptized members and the congregation to participate earnestly and meditatively in the litany.)

NEWLY BAPTIZED: Almighty God, my Father in heaven, I thank you for the indescribable gift[1] of salvation in Jesus Christ in my life. I pray that I will hold firmly the faith I have come to share in Christ Jesus till I see you face to face.[2]

CONGREGATION: We pray that you remember your baptism as a transformative act,[3] an act that confesses and affirms your belonging to Christ and to the community of believers.

NEWLY BAPTIZED: O Lord, as I reflect on my life I realize that I have sinned and done wrong in your sight. I have been wicked and have rebelled knowingly and unknowingly. I know I have turned away from your commands and laws.[4] O Lord, I come before you with a repentant heart; may you wipe away my sins that times of refreshing may come to me even as I profess my inner faith with my mouth to you in the presence of the community of believers.[5]

CONGREGATION: We pray that you remember your baptism as a transformative act, an act that confesses and affirms your belonging to Christ and to the community of believers.

PASTOR: Lord Jesus, I am convinced that your beloved daughter (son) _____ (name of newly baptized) has (have) been baptized in the name of the Father and of the Son and of the Holy Spirit, signifying her (his) genuine repentance and acceptance of Jesus Christ in her (his) life as her (his) personal Lord and Savior. As I stand before you as the representative of the Good Shepherd of the sheep[6] in this congregation _____ (specify the local congregation), I delight in reminding our dearest _____ (name) to remember that she (he) has devoted to an eternal covenant between herself (himself) and God, to be a disciple of Jesus Christ, to have faith in him and in no other.[7] Therefore, I remind you, dear sister (brother), in the name of Jesus Christ:

You did not undergo this baptismal rite as a way of going through a Christian religious ritual just because you happened to be born in a Christian family or due to peer pressures that all your friends are now initiated into Christian churches as members. Neither did you participate in the ordinance of baptism for the need of a certificate of baptism that is required for your enrollment in a Christian college, nor for the purpose of obtaining a marriage certificate from the church, as people often consider such as their reasons for undergoing the holy act of baptism.[8] But your baptism signifies "purification from sin, and the immersion signifies that we are dead to sin, and like Christ, have been buried and risen again."[9] Remember that baptism is a form of exorcism.[10] That you renounce "the Evil One and all the works he delights in."[11] To do so, you do not only depend on the prayers of others as many Christians today popularly rush to prayer warriors, prophesiers, witchcraft, or sorcery for immediate answers to their problems. But you are called, _____ (name), to deepen your faith through prayer, reading, and meditating on the Word of God and through your daily walk with the Lord, individually as well as with the community of believers.

I earnestly pray, O Lord, that you speak to your beloved _____ (name), that this act of initiation into the body of Christ is an undying pledge to a life of radical discipleship. For from this moment on, she (he) enters into a spiritual warfare "to fight against sin and slay it, even to . . . her (his) dying breath."[12] To this end, may the enabling power of the Holy Spirit sustain this precious soul in times of life's most critical circumstances of trials and tribulations, so as to be purified and refined as though in a refiner's fire that her (his) faith may be proved genuine and that she (he) may reflect the character of Christ, all for the glory of God.[13]

NEWLY BAPTIZED: O Lord, with a clear conscience, I am here before your presence this moment. Having been baptized on the prompting of the power of the Holy Spirit, with a decision to walk in "the Way of Life" and intentionally guard my soul to turn away from "the Way of Death."[14] Most precious Lord, no matter what situation I may encounter, grant me the grace and strength to endure the burdens of my earthly journey even at the cost of my life, if need be.

Congregation: We pray that you remember your baptism as a transformative act, an act that confesses and affirms your belonging to Christ and to the community of believers.

Newly Baptized: I pray for your enabling grace,[15] O Lord, that I may internalize the baptismal teachings of one baptism[16] for the forgiveness of sins. That in response, may I be aware of the grace that challenges me to forgive others *continually*[17] in the name of Jesus Christ, just as I have been graciously forgiven of my sins.[18] Help me that I may not only retain the teachings I have received in my mind but also efficiently live out through my *conduct*,[19] by way of resisting temptations of all sorts that *subtly* disengages me from building up a soul-sustaining relationship with you, O Lord.

Congregation: We pray that you remember your baptism as a transformative act, an act that confesses and affirms your belonging to Christ and to the community of believers.

Pastor: Almighty God, how heaven must be rejoicing today as one precious soul confessed before God and the church to have come to the knowledge of your saving grace![20] I commend to you, O Lord, both the newly baptized and the congregation of _____ (name the church) in the name of the Father and of the Son and of the Holy Spirit, that we may take upon ourselves the responsibilities of a true Christian. That from this day on, each of us, the community of believers will, *with intent*, nurture and support our precious sister (brother) to grow in the likeness of Christ Jesus our Lord and Savior.[21]

And all the people of God say:

Congregation: AMEN.

Baptism
ERIKA MARKSBURY

The waters are central to the story of our faith—they swirl at creation, they part to make a way for God's people seeking liberation, they anoint, they restore, and they are a symbol of blessing. At the beginning of our Gospel narratives, Jesus comes to the waters to dedicate himself to God's work, and there he is claimed and called beloved. He tells a woman beside a well about living water, he stills a storm at sea, and he washes the feet of his friends...

...for those reasons and more, when we want to say we believe, when we decide to commit ourselves to following Jesus, we come to the waters. In our tradition, this immersion is a way of saying, as you go under, that you die to an old way, a centeredness in self; and as you come back up, you rise into the way of Jesus, and into a centeredness in the presence of God that is in all of creation.

[Candidate Name], do you confess the God made known in Jesus, and through his teachings, and do you claim your identity as a beloved child of God? Do you come to these waters to commit to following the way of compassion, justice, and good news, modeled by Jesus?

[CANDIDATE]: I do.

[Candidate Name], in the name of God who loves you, Christ who walks beside you, and the Spirit who lives within you, I baptize you.

God, we give thanks for [Candidate Name], for the commitment *she/he* has made today, for the way your life and your love shine through *her/him*. May these waters be a blessing—may *she/he* know *herself/himself*, now and always, washed in your grace and upheld by your love. We give thanks for this community that surrounds *her/him*, claims *her/him* as one of their own, and calls *her/him* beloved, just as you do. Amen.

NOTES

1. 2 Corinthians 9:5: "Thanks be unto God for His indescribable gift" (NIV).
2. Hebrews 3:14: "We have come to share Christ if we hold firmly till the end the confidence we had at first." The NIV Study Bible interprets this verse as "salvation is evidenced by continuing in faith to the end."

3. Acts 2:38. "The gift of the Holy Spirit" is the indwelling transformational agent of God in a believer's life.

4. 1 Samuel 15:24, 25; Daniel 9:5; Psalm 51:4.

5. Romans 10:10.

6. Hebrews 13:20, 21; John 10:11.

7. Acts 4:12.

8. Sashinungla Pongen, *The Predicament of Christian Spirituality in Nagaland: 1947 to the Present: Historical Background, Cultural Identity, and Proposal for Change* (PhD Diss., Luther Seminary, May 2016), 26–28.

9. Acts 22:16; Romans 6:4. John A. Broadus, *A Catechism of Bible Teaching* (Philadelphia: American Baptist Publication Society and Sunday School Board of Southern Baptist Convention, 1892), 32: Archival Collection, BIM, American Baptist Historical Society, Atlanta, GA.

10. Thomas M. Finn, *Early Christian Baptism and the Catechumenate: West and East Syria,* vol. 5 of *Message of the Fathers of the Church* (Collegeville, MN: The Liturgical Press, 1992), General Introduction, 6.

11. Finn, *Early Christian Baptism,* 78.

12. Martin Luther, "The Holy and Blessed Sacrament of Baptism, 1519," in Word and Sacrament I (ed. E. Theodore Bachmann; vol. 35 of Luther's Works, American Edition, ed. Jaroslav Pelikan and Helmut T. Lehmann; Philadelphia: Fortress, 1970), 35.

13. Isaiah 43:2; 48:10; John 16:33; 1 Peter 1:6-9.

14. Aaron Milavec, *The Didache: Text, Translation, Analysis, and Commentary* (Collegeville, MN: Liturgical Press, 2003), 44–48, 52–55, 62–63.

15. Ephesians 2:8-10.

16. Ephesians 4:5, 6: "one Lord, one faith, one baptism; one God and Father of all, who is over and through all and in all."

17. Mathew 18:21-22.

18. Mathew 6:14, 15; Ephesians 4:32; Colossians 3:13.

19. Philippians 1:27, 28. The story of the early church tells us that "the early Christian was persuaded that conduct mirrored conviction." Finn, *Early Christian Baptism,* General Introduction, 5.

20. Luke 15:7.

21. Ephesians 4:12-16; 1 Thessalonians 2:7-12.

Remembering Baptism: Our Covenantal Beginnings
SHARON R. FENNEMA

*This ritual could take place with the community gathered around
the baptismal font or pool or using bowls of water set up around
the worship space. A worship leader or dancers could pour water
into the font, pool, or bowls as each of the three leader parts is
being read and/or during the prayer to further enhance the sensory
experience.*

SUNG REFRAIN: Wade in the Water
TEXT & MUSIC: African American Spiritual

>*Wade in the water.*
>*Wade in the water, children.*
>*Wade in the water.*
>*God's gonna trouble the water.*

LEADER: In the beginning, there is water.
Chaotic, spirit-hovered-over, love-stirred-up water,
the water from which all creation was birthed
the water that makes up our bodies, courses through
    our veins
the water that dried up so that slaves could cross over
    to freedom.
This is the water that we use to bless one another, to
    baptize.
This same water calls each one of us "beloved"
This same water welcomes each body to the Body of
    Christ,
the water of the covenant-promise that teaches us
to see our neighbor:
those who abide in love abide in God and God abides in
    them.

SUNG REFRAIN: Wade in the Water
TEXT & MUSIC: African American Spiritual,
            adpt. Avery R. Young

>*Lead in the water.*
>*Lead in the water, children.*
>*Lead in the water.*
>*Someone's playing God with the water.*

LEADER: In the meantime, there is water.
Polluted, wars-fought-over, struggle-stirred-up water,

the water that flooded the earth
     threatening to extinguish all life
     giving birth to rainbow covenants
the water stolen from rivers and lakes
to feed golf courses and capitalist thirst
the water that poisons communities of color.
This is the water that we use to bless one another, to
    baptize.
This same water calls each one of us "beloved"
This same water welcomes each body to the Body of
    Christ,
the water of the covenant-promise that teaches us
to hear our neighbor:
those who abide in love abide in God and God abides in
    them.

SUNG REFRAIN: Wade in the Water
TEXT & MUSIC: African American Spiritual, adpt.

> *Love in the water.*
> *Love in the water, children.*
> *Love in the water.*
> *Witness to the Love in the water.*

LEADER: At this moment, there is water,
Precious, prayed-over, promise-stirred-up water.
You are invited to come to this water,
to remember your baptism
or the promises of steadfast love made to you
    at the foundation of the world,
        whether you are baptized or not.
Be troubled by the water to trouble the waters of fear,
    hate, and prejudice.
Witness to the Love that flows abundantly from the
    Source.
This is the water that we use to bless one another, to
    baptize.
This same water calls each one of us "beloved"
This same water welcomes each body to the Body of
    Christ,
the water of the covenant-promise that teaches us
to love our neighbor:
those who abide in love abide in God and God abides in
    them.

BAPTISM SERVICE

LEADER: Let us pray:
Blessed are you, Holy One, our God,
who gathered up the waters of creation
     so that life might spring forth on the earth,

ASSEMBLY: who leads us out of the water that nourishes our births and rebirths,

LEADER: who used water-soaked feet-washing to show us our servant callings,

ASSEMBLY: who drenches us with grace and calls us beloved,
using our diverse lives and our unique gifts
in the unfolding story of salvation and new life.

LEADER: Come to us, Water of Life, and pour out your Spirit among us,

ASSEMBLY: trouble this water so that it might hold our
remembrance of the past,
our work in the present,
and our dreams of the future.
Amen.

Worshipers are then invited to go to the font, pool, or one of the bowls of water near them, to place their hands in the water, to touch their foreheads or face with the water of life. If leaders are present at the font, pool, or bowl of water, they can address each person saying, "Remember that you are God's unique and beloved child; remember that we are one by the grace of God." The community could continue to sing "Wade in the Water" as people make their way through the space. Bowls of water could also be brought around the gathering for those who are unable to access the font, pool, or bowls of water.

Litany to Remember We Are Baptized
DON NG
Based on Ephesians 4:4-6

LEADER: Martin Luther once said that when he felt himself sinking into the depths of despair, he found it helpful to touch his forehead where the sign of the cross had been made at his baptism, and to say, "I am baptized." Remembrance of his baptism recalled for Luther God's determined ownership of him, and this provided comfort in distress.

In light of Ephesians 4:4-6, let's take our cue from Martin Luther, and in the face of divisions, let us touch our foreheads, and repeat the words, "I am baptized." This means that there is "one Lord, one faith, one baptism"; therefore, we have the gift of unity.

LEADER: In the church, when we are addressing the sin of racism, remember:

PEOPLE: I am baptized. I am not bound by the traditional categories of insiders and outsiders. The old, painful external distinctions made between people have been washed away in the waters of baptism.

LEADER: In struggling with injustices committed against women through the ages and still today, remember:

PEOPLE: I am baptized. "There is neither male nor female" in Christ. Gender is not the fundamental identity of Christians.

LEADER: When living in a world where people are often judged by the clothes they wear, the kind of automobiles they drive, and the size of their houses, remember:

PEOPLE: I am baptized. The deep distinctions between rich and poor, haves and have-nots, have been rearranged and disrupted in Christ so that we come to see those of us who are rich-in-things are often poor-in-spirit, and those of us who are poor-in-things are often rich-in-spirit.

ALL: I am baptized. This makes all the difference.

The Dedication of a Child by the Family of God
Central Baptist Church, Wayne, PA[1]

PASTOR: "Whoever welcomes in my Name one of these children, welcomes me, and whoever welcomes me, welcomes not only me but the One who sent me." [Mark 9:36-37]

[*to the parents*] Will you now dedicate yourselves to your child?

PARENTS: "We will tell our child of the wonderful acts which God has performed so that s/he will place her/his trust in God." [Psalms 78:4, 7]

We praise God for this life that has been entrusted to our care. We covenant to nurture our child in the church, in the Word of God, in prayer, and by the example of our lives. We recognize that the gift of faithfulness to Christ can be life's riches blessing. We pray that blessing this day for _____ (name of child).

PASTOR: [*to the sponsors*] Will you now dedicate yourselves to this child?

SPONSORS: The promises by a congregation must be made real by the actions of individuals within it. We stand today with this child, expressing our commitment to the faithful nurture of _____ (name of child).

PASTOR: [*to the congregation*] Will you please stand and dedicate yourselves to this child?

PEOPLE: We stand here today to speak as a congregation and to represent the church wherever and whenever it will serve this child, to dedicate ourselves, our congregation, and the church universal to its care and keeping, toward faith that heals and unites. We will be advocates as s/he grows as a child exploring the wonder of the created world. We will be loving and forgiving as s/he matures as an adolescent, in victory, in searching, in finding.

We will be a community of fellow pilgrims as s/he ventures through the adult years, giving of herself/ himself toward the reign of God.

And when her/his life on earth comes to an end, this same body of believers will be there to testify to the eternity of God's love in which s/he will be raised to fulfillment and wholeness. [*Please be seated*]

PASTOR: [*to the children*] Will you please stand and dedicate yourselves to this child?

CHILDREN: We stand today to welcome this child and to offer our friendship as we learn, grow, and play together. Together we will explore, discover, and learn. We will ask questions, look for answers, and grow. With this child, we will share our love, our faith, and our playthings.

PASTOR: [*Blessing and Prayer of Dedication*]

DEDICATION OF A CHILD SERVICE

Prayer of Invocation
JENNIFER W. DAVIDSON

Holy One, who fires our hearts anew
with your astounding love,
send your Spirit into this place of worship now
that we might be reinvigorated
with our thirst to know you,
recommitted to the waters of our baptism,
and renewed in our desire to share your Good News
with every seeking soul.
We ask in the name of the One
who in his dying, defeated death
and in his rising, gifted true life.
Amen.

Prayer of Opening
JENNIFER W. DAVIDSON

All-knowing and all-caring God,
we gather this day,
weary from our work.
We are like a parched desert,
empty and in need of replenishment.
Visit us with your presence,
saturate us with your Spirit,
and bathe us in your streams of living water,
that our lives might acknowledge and worship you
to the praise and honor of Jesus Christ. **Amen!**
—based on John 4:13-14; 7:37-38

NOTE

1. The Uncommon Book of Worship, 4th ed. (Wayne, PA: Central Baptist Church, 1997)

FEAST OF GRACE

CHAPTER 7

COMMUNION AS WELCOMING, EMBODYING, AND SUSTAINING

Remember how we took bread and made it
    meaningful?
Now look at this. This moment can be
    meaningful as well.
We can see, in this ordinary moment, that
    God is present.

—Don Ng[1]

EVERY SUNDAY WHEN I was growing up, there was one particular pew in our church that was pretty well filled with members of my extended family. But on the first Sunday of every month, there was one seat empty on our pew. My grandfather never came to church on communion Sundays. I don't know why. It wasn't something anyone ever talked about. But as the years went by, I would feel his absence keenly. Why did he never attend worship on those Sundays? Was it a sense of unworthiness? Was it some strong principle that kept him from worship on those days? Mind you, he didn't just sit in the pew and choose not to receive communion. He wouldn't come to worship at all.

In a strange way, it struck me as one of the most faithful acts I ever knew my grandfather to take. It's not like he talked about his faith. He would say grace at the table, but I always had the sense that was only because my grandmother made him do it. But his absence on communion Sundays suggested to me that his faith ran deep, even if it was expressed more as a kind of brokenness and resistance than any kind of traditional piety.

My grandfather's persistent absence from communion somehow taught me its profound importance and its heightened meaning more than everyone else's consistent attendance. I perceived a weightiness to communion precisely because my grandfather couldn't bring himself to the table. What is it about communion, I wondered, that was powerful enough to keep him away? But I perceived power in my grandfather's resistance to communion as well; I figured he had to be strong to hold communion at bay.

The weightiness of communion and this strange strength I perceived in my grandfather caused me to become self-reflective (likely to a fault) about my own worthiness to receive communion. "We are not worthy to gather the crumbs from beneath thy table, O Lord," our pastor would intone every Lord's Supper. I would descend into my heart and investigate whether I felt worthy to come to the table myself. If I were angry with someone or knew there was a broken relationship in my life, then I stayed in my seat when others went forward. I came to think of this as a form of fasting. I took it to heart that I risked my very soul if I were to receive communion in error. I trembled in fear when I thought of Paul's warning: "The one eating and drinking not discerning the body, eats and drinks judgment on [her]self" (1 Corinthians 11:29). For me, communion was a meal of judgment long before it was ever a meal of grace.[2]

I shared this story recently with a former seminary professor of mine, Bob Robinson. "I suspect there are a lot of people who can relate to that feeling," he mused. Bob volunteers at his church's homelessness mission in downtown Philadelphia where he helps serve breakfast every Saturday morning. It's common for men from the church's shelter to come to worship on Sunday mornings. "But," he told me, "the men from the mission who come to worship never come up and receive communion, no matter how many times I've encouraged them to do so." Their reasons, like those of my grandfather, are complicated, I imagine, and for the most part, they are unknown to my friend. But it's ironic that confronting one's own sense of worthlessness is often a profound barrier to approaching the table where, of all things, the feast of grace is made available to all. Sometimes it really does take all of our strength to resist a gift freely given. I know from experience.

And yet, as my friend Bob is talking, I can't help but think of the breakfast served to these very same men on Saturday mornings. I hear words from Jesus that unravel the idea that communion only ever happens in worship on the first Sunday of the month: "As often as you do this, do it in remembrance of me" (1 Corinthians 11:24-26).

What distinguishes one meal from the next? In some ways the answer is obvious. The communion meal is ritualized, accompanied by specific prayers, and happens in the context of a Sunday morning worship service. The meal that is designated as communion is symbolic, represented by little portions of bread and tiny cups of grape juice; whereas, the men's breakfast happens in the hubbub of Saturday morning, surrounded by the coats, socks, shoes, and other clothing that get distributed each week. On Saturday morning the meal is eaten around tables and amid noisy conversations. It's not a symbolic meal, but a real one. (It may well be the only real meal the men will get that day.) No one would call it worship, exactly. And yet, I think we impoverish our theology if we draw too sharp a distinction between these two meals. Maybe if the congregation and the men themselves understood Saturday morning breakfast as part of communion, then that otherwise insurmountable wall would come crashing down on Sunday morning.

Even as I continued to fast from communion on some Sundays, especially in my late teens and early twenties, I also began to see communion everywhere. Over coffee and donuts in the morning, at dinner with friends, even sometimes with nothing more than chips and soda. When those moments included searching questions of faith and invited Jesus' presence in our midst through shared struggles and hopes, I discovered communion. I sensed a transcendence in those meals that, to be honest, didn't often happen for me in a worship service even when we did celebrate communion.

It's nothing short of a gift that in the years when I felt least worthy to approach the table of grace during communion, God opened my eyes to see that God's grace is offered to us at *every* table, whenever and wherever food and drink are shared. This paradox is something we'll try to keep in mind throughout this conversation about the theological meanings of communion—the ordinariness and the extraordinariness of the meal. If we can keep both in mind, it will actually tell us something about how God works. It's all there in the incarnation: the extraordinariness of the Divine crammed into the ordinariness of Jesus, a first-century Jew living under Roman occupation in the backwaters of Galilee.

WELCOMING

What do you do to help others feel welcome at your home when you invite them to dinner? Chances are you prepare the space for them, probably taking time to clean your home with more attention than usual. You might check in with your guests as you plan the meal, making sure there are no allergies or ingredients that are strongly disliked. You probably set the table a little differently, maybe with special dishes for the occasion, or at the very least adding enough place settings for everyone you expect.

In our house, we often need to clear piles of mail from the dining room table, so we have enough space for everyone to join us! We will also take a little time before the meal starts to describe to our guests how we pray together before the meal. We take one another's hands and say together in unison: "Thank you, God, who is our bread. May all the world be clothed and fed." Then we each name specific people or situations that we especially want to lift up in prayer, going around the table one by one. We tell our guests that they may close their eyes or keep them open; they may pray aloud or not at all. The only required part, we explain, is that we all hold hands.

While we might be accustomed to always thinking of communion as a reenactment of Jesus' *last* supper with his disciples on the evening before his crucifixion, in fact the meaning of communion encompasses all of Jesus' table ministry. With whom did Jesus eat? Who did he welcome at the table? At whose houses did Jesus eat? When we look at Jesus' dining practices, we discover that he consistently shared meals with sinners, tax collectors, outcasts, women, and people with poor reputations.

In his table ministry Jesus upended notions about who is worthy and who is not. Dalit theologian Peniel Rajkumar[3] asserts that Jesus' table fellowship is just as important as his healing ministry, because both ministries reveal to us God's central character.[4] When we pay attention to who Jesus healed, and who Jesus shared meals with, we discover God's radical, boundary-crossing love for the world.

> The radical nature of the compassion of Jesus can be seen in his violation of the social codes of exclusion. The inclusive nature of the healings proclaim the unconditional and non-discriminatory nature of God's love. Jesus' willingness to cross boundaries to touch and cleanse and eat with the outcast ones ushered in life and hope where there was none. It was a threatening willingness which sought to rock the very foundations of the whole religious and cultural and political system by which life is ordered. It was Jesus' concern for these marginal people that made him a matter of concern to those who are in charge.[5]

Jesus' practices of eating with and healing outcasts reveal God's intentions of ending segregation, disrupting caste-ism and classism, and valuing *most highly* those who are considered by society to be most impure, unholy, or unvalued.

When we understand communion in the light of *all* the meals Jesus shared, we discover that communion is a radically welcoming act. But even if we choose only Jesus' final meal as our model for a theology of communion, we still can see evidence of radical welcome. At that last supper, Jesus shared the bread and cup not only with his most beloved and faithful disciples, but also with the disciple who would betray him, the disciple who would deny him, and the disciples who would fall asleep and run away. "If we can only come to the table when we are sure we are perfect," Khalia Jelks Williams

SACRAMENT VERSUS ORDINANCE:
A WORD ABOUT LANGUAGE

It was Augustine's reflections on the sacraments that eventually gave rise to the widely accepted definition of the term sacrament as "the outward and visible sign of an inward and invisible grace." In his chapter on "Baptism and the Lord's Supper as Community Acts," theologian Stanley Grenz recounted the history of how Anabaptists and some English Baptists came to eschew the term sacrament altogether and replace it with the term ordinance.

Grenz explained that by the time of the Reformation, the church had come to understand a sacrament as "a cause of grace" that was effective "without regard to the spiritual condition of either the participant or the administrator of the sacrament."[1] Radical reformers felt the term had become so theologically misleading that it needed to be removed from the church's vocabulary.[2] They settled on the term ordinance, because baptism and communion were both "ordained" (commanded) by Jesus for his followers to observe. Most Baptists today refer to communion and baptism as "ordinances."

Yet Grenz urged his readers to reclaim a more sacramental and communal understanding of baptism and communion, referring to them as "the church's rites" that "carry sacramental significance in that they are identity-conveying and identity-forming events."[3] Through our participation in these rites as a church, we remember God's saving acts on our behalf in the past and we celebrate the eschatological vision of God's hope for our future. "As we are en-storied in this manner—as we are caught up into both God's past action in Christ and the vision of God's future—we find purpose and meaning for our own lives, for we gain a sense of the connectedness of all history, and we come to see our present within the flow of God's story."[4]

Likewise advocating for a reclamation of the term sacrament, Baptist theologian Clark Pinnock suggested that Baptists need a much more expansive definition of the term. It is possible to see God's grace mediated—conveyed, communicated, made real and alive to us—through

reflects, "that's going to be a very small, very exclusive table. But that's not what Jesus' table looked like."

Marcus Pomeroy agrees, "My encouragement, when I gave the invitation to the table at communion, was always to tell people they don't need to be in a right place. The invitation is for us to come in whatever place we are in, and to celebrate the fact that this body, this communion, this oneness, embraces us all. There is no earning it. We don't have to earn it." Tim Phillips, pastor of First Baptist Church of Seattle, inexhaustible sources. "God is everywhere and in everything," Pinnock wrote. "As Paul said, 'In him we live and move and have our being' (Acts 17:28). God is not far from anyone and his call goes out to everyone. Encountering the created world, persons experience God's presence."[5]

Pinnock suggested that a more expansive understanding of the term sacrament can help us see God and grace made alive for us not only in baptism and communion, but also in preaching, singing, praying, and the reading of Scripture. More than that, we can perceive God's living presence in much more ordinary moments like coffee hour, hospital visits, sitting with a friend who needs us, and in an encounter with a stranger on the street. "Recovering the sense of the sacramental is part of the renewal the churches need."[6] Pinnock concluded with the following plea:

> Christians have almost always seen sacraments as a means of grace. They have seen them not merely as acts of human obedience but as events where God moves. Let us not repudiate sacraments because we have misunderstood them or impoverished ourselves by over-reacting to flawed practices. We must not repudiate embodied means of grace. Sacraments are events where God acts to transform us and where people respond. [God] wants to grace our lives in multiple ways and communicate [God's] love for us.[7]

~~~

NOTES

1. Stanley Grenz, "Baptism and the Lord's Supper as Community Acts: Toward a Sacramental Understanding of the Ordinances," in *Baptist Sacramentalism, Studies in Baptist History and Thought*, vol. 5, ed. Anthony R. Cross and Philip E. Thompson (Waynesboro, GA: Paternoster Press, 2003), 77–78.

2. Grenz, 79.

3. Grenz, 90.

4. Grenz, 92.

5. Clark H. Pinnock, "The Physical Side of Being Spiritual: God's Sacramental Presence," in *Baptist Sacramentalism, Studies in Baptist History and Thought*, vol. 5, ed. Anthony R. Cross and Philip E. Thompson (Waynesboro, GA: Paternoster Press, 2003), 11.

6. Pinnock, 19.

7. Pinnock, 19–20.

puts it succinctly, "Communion is an invitation to anybody who feels the need to experience grace in their lives."

EMBODYING

A famous public advertising campaign in the United States in the early 1970s used clever cartoons and songs to encourage kids to eat healthfully. In one ad, a cartoon character sings: "You are what you eat, from your head down to your feet."[6]

As silly as it may seem, I remembered this ad from my childhood when I was a student at Lutheran Theological Seminary at Philadelphia twenty years ago. Gordon Lathrop, my wonderful liturgy professor, would preside at communion a few times a year. On occasion, when we would go up to receive the bread, he would place a large chunk of the bread in our open palms and say, while looking fiercely into our eyes: "The body of Christ: receive what you are." It was an astounding reminder for me as I ate the bread: We are what we eat; we are the Body of Christ.

Actually, the idea that "you are what you eat" goes back to 1826 when Jean Anthelme Brillat-Savarin wrote in his 7-volume work *The Physiology of Taste*, "Tell me what kind of food you eat and I will tell you what kind of man you are."[7] Brillat-Savarin had observed that the food people ate together at meals was an indicator of their social class and their social values.[8] When we study how people eat together at everyday occasions, big feasts, and ritualized meals like communion, we can understand what is important to a culture, how social relationships are constructed, and how a group understands belonging.[9]

Joseph Kutter, former pastor and executive director of the American Baptist Ministers Council, has noted the connection between baptism, belonging, and communion. "When I am baptized in the name of God, Christ, and the Holy Spirit, I am immersing myself in the totality of God. And that means I am immersing myself in God's mission for the world," he begins. "God loved the world. God has no interest in condemning the world. God's mission for the world is to make the world whole, to make it right, to make the world *shalom*.

"Now if that is what baptism is about," Joe continues, "then every time I take a piece of bread and drink the cup, I remember that this means in some profound way that the life of Christ is living in me; therefore, the *mission* of Christ is alive in me. Anybody who tries to do the mission of Christ without social justice just doesn't get it."

Participating in the meal means we ought not leave the table unchanged. Over and over again, month after month, we become the Body of Christ. We become what we are. We embody Christ. And the Body of Christ is always being broken and poured out for the sake of the world. Womanist theologian M. Shawn Copeland calls this *eucharistic solidarity*. "To put it compactly, embodying Christ is discipleship, and discipleship is embodied praxis. . . . Eucharistic solidarity challenges us in living out the implications and demands of discipleship."[10]

Though we may each receive (and become) the body of Christ, discipleship happens in community.[11] "Not only does Christ live in me, but Christ lives among *us* and within *us*," Joe Kutter explains, placing an emphasis on the word *us* every time he says it. "Christ's mission is with us, among us, for us. Frankly, when we signed up for church, we signed up for that mission." In other words, the meal we share together simultaneously reveals, shapes, and emboldens our communal values. Joe goes on:

> I think we try to get Christ without the mission. Somehow or other we have reduced salvation to a solitary solipsism, just-you-and-me Jesus, please get me to heaven if you can. But to separate God's heavenly kingdom from the rest of God's kingdom, I just think it's heresy. God's mandate is that those made in the image of God should have food, clothing, shelter, health insurance, education. Why would God create somebody for this world and then say to that person, "Oh, by the way, I'm not going to give you the resources you need to become a full-grown human being?" It's contrary to God's character; so, when we try to be Christian without that, we miss the essence of who God is.

The questions that are posed to us, then, as we come to the table and eat the food that becomes us are these: Are we, like Jesus, being broken and poured out for the sake of the world?

Are we leaving this meal as ones who have been transformed?
Are we, really, the body of Christ?

SUSTAINING

In the United States, eating is a very conflicted thing. Food is
simultaneously nothing more than a form of fuel to keep the
body alive and efficient, and a source of almost devilish pleasure.[12] As fuel, food is reduced to caloric content and stripped
of its joy and communal value. Yet as source of pleasure,
food is often understood as guilt-inducing or "sinful." We
need only look at a dessert menu to be convinced: chocolate
decadence, death by chocolate, chocolate fantasy, and even
devil's food cake! Lord, lead me not into temptation!

Michelle Stacey writes:

> Obsessing about food is more than a national pastime;
> it's on its way to becoming a national disorder. Dieticians
> are beginning to jettison ideas of 'eating normally' in the
> face of almost universal dieting and a pattern they term
> 'restrained eating'—eating not in response to natural cues
> of hunger but to external cues of will and self-control.
> Indeed, control is key in this new way of eating; food is
> transformed from a source of pleasure and sustenance to a
> test of resolve and a wellspring of power, moral superiority,
> even class status.[13]

Michael Pollan has made a convincing case that North
Americans are especially conflicted about food because of the
influences of both nutrition science and the food industry.
"As eaters we find ourselves increasingly in the grip of a Nutritional Industrial Complex—comprised of well-meaning, if
error-prone, scientists—and food marketers only too eager to
exploit every shift in the nutritional consensus."[14] As we have
become more informed about the food we are eating, many of
us feel more confused than ever about what to eat, how much
to eat, and whether it's okay to enjoy any of it! While we may
think that focusing on food solely as a matter of nutrients

would be the healthiest outlook, in fact, separating food from its spiritual significance and communal richness makes us less healthy. "Indeed, no people on earth worry more about the health consequences of their food choices than we Americans do—and no people suffer from as many diet-related health problems. We are becoming a nation of orthorexics: people with an unhealthy obsession with healthy eating."[15]

Although the bread and cup on a communion table obviously do not provide us with a balanced diet, they do serve as reminders that God is concerned with both our physical and spiritual needs. The commonness of the elements is meant to connect this transcendent moment in worship to our everyday moments. At the same time, we can connect our everyday moments, such as when we gather around a kitchen table with family or a dining table with friends, back to transcendent moments when we are aware of God's presence. Don Ng, former president of American Baptist Churches, USA, and longtime pastor of First Chinese Baptist Church in San Francisco, puts it this way:

> "It all kind of converges. If it's true that there becomes something sacred about this piece of bread and this cup of juice or wine, then there are other things in ordinary life that can be extraordinary. The mundane becomes the supra-mundane. I saw this as an important part of my ministry, to say: 'Remember how we took bread and made it meaningful? Now look at this. This moment can be meaningful as well. We can see, in this ordinary moment, that God is present.'"

We need a sense of God's presence in our everyday lives to truly be fed, to be sustained for the long road of discipleship. The meal that is communion is a dramatic reminder that God seeks to nourish and sustain us. It is a reminder that we need God to live just as we need food to live. It is a reminder that food adds joy and enjoyment to our lives, and that God desires joy and enjoyment in life. As if God knew about junk food long before the food industry existed, God lamented,

"Why do you spend your money for that which is not bread, and your labor for that which does not satisfy?" And God invited, "Listen carefully to me, and eat what is good, and delight yourselves in rich food" (Isaiah 55:2). The distinction between our physical sustenance and our spiritual sustenance disappears altogether as God continues to speak through Isaiah's voice: "Incline your ear, and come to me; listen, so that you may live" (Isaiah 55:3a).

We need to be reminded, as often as possible but at least once a month, that God promises to sustain us for the journey. This is a reason God gave us communion. We do not approach the communion meal full of resolve or concerned about calories, but we approach with open hands. We do not come to the table as if we need nothing, but we approach fully aware of our need. We come with empty hands and open hearts saying, "We need you, God. We cannot do this without you." And we hear God saying back to us, "Yes, you do need me, beloved ones. You cannot do this without me, so I give myself to you. Come and eat. Be filled."

NOTES

1. Don Ng, interview by author, Berkeley, CA, 2017.

2. The soul-wrenching worry about whether or not one is worthy to approach the table is not a new thing. In his book *Meeting House to Camp Meeting: Toward a History of American Free Church Worship from 1620–1835*, Doug Adams points to the distinction made between "the church (persons with a regenerative experience that qualified them for church membership and communion) and the congregation (persons without a regenerative experience and unqualified for membership or communion even if they had been baptized)." See *Meeting House* (Saratoga, NY and Austin, TX: Modern Liturgy-Resource Publications and The Sharing Company, 1981), 84. The British Congregationalist Solomon Stoddard spoke against this practice of distinguishing between communicants and non-communicants, and further noted that "If the Lord's Supper be only for the strengthening of Saints, then they who are not Saints and do not profane the Ordinance, when they do partake, and it is not Lawful for them to partake, and then they do not know themselves to be Saints, don't know that it is Lawful for them to partake, and so far as any Man hath scruples about his Saintship, he must proportionably have scruples about the Lawfulness of his Participation, and so Sacrament Days which should be Days of Comfort, will become Days of Torment." Solomon Stoddard, *The Doctrine of Instituted Churches, Explained and Proved from the Word of God* (London: Printed for Ralph Smith, at the Bible under the Piazza of Exchange in Cornhil, 1700), 22, https://play.google.com/store/books/details?id=wdUCAAAAQAAJ&hl=en.

3. "Dalit theology is a form of liberation theology which addresses the issue of the liberation of Dalit communities from caste-based discrimination...The term

'Dalit' is the name by which several communities who were previously known as the 'untouchables' prefer to be known today. This is because the term 'Dalit' captures the spirit of struggle amid persistent brokenness." See Peniel Jesudason Rufus Rajkumar, "Dalit theology: the 'untouched' touching theology," in *Asian Theology on the Way: Christianity, Culture, and Context*, ed. Peniel Rajkumar (Minneapolis, MN: Fortress Press, 2015), 132.

4. See Peniel Rajkumar, *Dalit Theology and Dalit Liberation: Problems, Paradigms, and Possibilities* (New York: Routledge Press, 2016), 92–94.

5. Peniel Rajkumar, 109.

6. ABC Television, "Time for Timer: You Are What You Eat" (Public Service Announcement), https://youtu.be/QoitR0gFVfE.

7. Jaan Anthelme Brillat-Savarin, *Physiology of Taste: Or Meditations on Transcendental Gastronomy*, trans. Fayette Robinson (Philadelphia: Lindsay & Blakiston, 1854), 25.

8. Tamara Kohn summarizes it this way: "Tell me what and how you eat and I'll tell you how your society is organised and given meaning." See "Stuffed Turkey and Pumpkin Pie: In, Through and Out of American Contexts," *Cultural Studies Review* 19, no. 1 (March 2013): 50, http://dx.doi.org/10.5130/csr.v19i1.3075.

9. Kohn, 50.

10. M. Shawn Copeland, *Enfleshing Freedom: Body, Race, and Being* (Minneapolis: Fortress Press, 2009), 127–128.

11. Another way to say this is that community/communion is necessary for faithful discipleship, for solidarity.

12. See Patrick McCormick, "How Could We Break the Lord's Bread in a Foreign Land? The Eucharist in 'Diet America,'" *Horizons* 25.1 (Spring 1998): 43-57.

13. Michelle Stacey, *Consumed: Why Americans Love, Hate, and Fear Food* (New York: Touchstone, 1994), 172.

14. Michael Pollan, *In Defense of Food: An Eater's Manifesto* (New York: Penguin Books, 2008), 7–8.

15. Pollan, 8–9.

CHAPTER 8

COMMUNION AS CONNECTING, HOPING, REMEMBERING, AND SENDING

> Entering into divine life is impossible unless we also
> enter into a life of love and communion with others.
> —Catherine LaCugna[1]

CONNECTING

B ECAUSE IT IS a shared meal, communion reminds us
that we cannot go through this life alone. We need the
companionship of others who also gather at the table
for food. Communion is a feast, even if represented symboli-
cally in only the presence of bread and wine or juice. A feast
cannot be eaten alone; it needs others to make it a feast.[2]
The biblical scholar James Brenneman points out, "Nineteen
times when the Greek word for 'communion' (*koinonia*) is
used in the New Testament it is variously translated as 'fellowship,' 'sharing,' 'contributing to others,' 'participation
with others,' having things 'in common,' 'in communion.'"[3]
By sharing in communion, we become connected with others
who share the same meal. We become *community*.

This understanding is essential to Marcus Pomeroy, who
often uses the words *communion* and *congregation* inter-
changeably. "Communion is not an individualistic thing,"
he tells me. "We *are* a communion. God calls a *people*. We

are called not so much into a personal identity as we are into a communal identity. When we gather in worship, we aren't celebrating our individuality, but our commonality, our connection."

As we have mentioned earlier, the community formed around the table in worship is not an idealized one. The communion table is surrounded by broken people who gather around broken bread. "I think we shouldn't forget," says Debora Jackson, director of lifelong learning at Yale Divinity School, "that Jesus was building community and sustaining relationship and fellowship with people who would ultimately betray him; therefore, we have a responsibility to keep connections even with people that we might disagree with."

Khalia Jelks Williams explains that two things happen at once in communion. "It welcomes everything about who we are, especially for those of us who must battle daily with oppression and messages that say we don't measure up. Communion becomes the space where God reminds us that we are enough." But at the same time, Khalia says, at the table "God allows us to see one another for who we really are— oppressors and oppressed. Both are made in the image of God." Often these are not hard-and-fast categories, but fluid ones. Each one gathered at God's table, each one welcomed by God, might potentially be both oppressor and oppressed. M. Shawn Copeland reminds us that the communion table is a place "where we grasp the enormity of suffering, affliction, and oppression as well as apprehend our complicity in the suffering, affliction, and oppression of others."[4]

In the earliest churches, the practice of communion was a radical reordering of communal relationships so that all could be cared for and fed. This is why Paul was so troubled by the disordered relationships on display in 1 Corinthians 11, when the wealthiest would arrive at the meal early, eat their fill, drink until they were drunk, and leave nothing for those who had to work late. As Neil Elliot points out, "The common meal is not really the Lord's Supper so long as some remain hungry when the meal is over. The disaster in Corinth was that the prosperous failed to make any connection between their worship and the poverty in their midst."[5] The common meal confronts us with our failure to embody true community, our failure to care for the least of these. At the same time, the common meal also provides a transformative vision of what true community really can look like, and a yearning that it might become our reality. In this sense, communion is simultaneously judgment and grace.

HOPING

Worship happens in the context of community, says the British liturgical theologian Christopher Ellis, but its horizon, or its focal point, is always beyond the community toward God's future.[6] Communion is eschatological in that it is oriented toward God's future and, as such, is suffused in hope. It is "a future orientation which hopes that God will act here and now, but which is always looking beyond the here and now."[7] An authentic eschatology is relentlessly honest about the conditions of injustice and brokenness in the world today, and equally relentless about imagining a world in which the vision of God's kin-dom comes into being.

It may be a challenge for us to perceive the future focus of our communion practices because we tend to think of the Lord's Supper first as a memorial—remembering what happened on the night Jesus was betrayed. How can our memory of an event in the past have a future orientation? But when we worship, we are inserted into a space that is between memory and hope.[8] We remember what God has done for us in the past, and we anticipate with hope what God will do in the future, God's reconciliation of all things (Colossians 1:15-23). Through our proclamation of Scripture, our preaching, our singing, and our practices of baptism and communion, we remember what God has done in the past, we affirm what God is doing in the present, and we remember what God has promised to do in the future.[9] In our recollection and our anticipation, we welcome God into our present moment.[10] We are transformed by the presence of God so that the world can likewise be transformed.

At the time of communion, we remember together a tragedy. We remember when the Son of God was murdered by the world God dearly loved. And yet, thanks be to God, our memory does not stop there. Because through communion we also remember God's ultimate "No" to death; or, to rephrase it, we remember God's ultimate "Yes" to life through the resurrection. We remember with great rejoicing that God's response to Jesus' death was not to put an end to those of us who would undo God, but to put an end to the finality of death. In response to our attempts to undo God, God instead undoes death.

Just as our baptism is our participation in Jesus' death in such a way that we are freed to a fullness of life, so communion is the repeated reminder that we need not fear death, nor are we to be enamored with it. Through Christ we are liberated from the grip of death so we can fully embrace life.

It is important, therefore, to keep in mind that at the time of communion we are not *only* remembering a tragedy. We are remembering more than that! Andrea Bieler and Luise Schottroff use the term *eschatological anamnesis* to convey the fullness of what we remember in our practice of communion.[11] The Greek term *anamnesis* is translated as "remembrance" in Scripture when Jesus commands, "Do this in remembrance of me." Bieler and Schottroff warn that by focusing exclusively on remembering Jesus' death, we neglect to remember Jesus' lowly birth, his ministry to the marginalized and oppressed, his feeding of the hungry, his challenge to the religious leaders and the politically powerful, and his resistance to empire. "Remembering Christ's ministry to the poor and marginalized is not a nostalgia with no connection to the present; it can rather inspire us to become aware of how Christ's saving and healing presence is at work today and how we can participate in it."[12]

Eschatological anamnesis is, therefore, more than a mental activity. It becomes an active practice that aligns us to God's saving work in the world today, allows us to touch our own places of pain and grief, abolishes apathy, and creates empathy for others who struggle.[13] Such practice helps create hopeful connection and solidarity. It takes courage, because it requires a fierce honesty about the pain that continues to be inflicted in the world today through racism, classism, hetero-sexism, white supremacy, ableism, and so on. It takes courage because it requires a vulnerability that can come only through imagining and hoping in a world that can be different.

Christopher Ellis reminds us that all of worship has this eschatological focus:

> Worship must be God-centered, but it also needs to be Kingdom-focused. The worshipper should not only be lost in love for God, but discover a passion for God's Kingdom to come and God's will to be done. The love of God should lead to the love of neighbour as expressed in Jesus's summing up of the law (Mark 12:28-31). Here is both rest and movement, relationship and action—communion, dialogue, and petition.[14]

REMEMBERING

We didn't plan to hold a communion service in the middle of a parking lot on a cold and damp December night in 2014. We also didn't plan on being arrested. But both were happening. It was the third night of protests in the streets of Oakland and Berkeley, California, after news had broken that there would be no indictments for the death of Eric Garner, who had been choked to death by a New York City police officer while being arrested earlier that year. The number of protesters had grown exponentially for several nights, as we walked nearly ten miles a night through city streets, crying out in communal lament the names of women and men who had been killed by police locally and nationally. A group of about twenty students and faculty members from the seminaries at the Graduate Theological Union were participating together in that night's protests, many of us wearing clothing or carrying signs that identified us as people of faith and clergy.

At several points throughout the evening, especially as tensions were rising between peaceful protestors and anxious police, we began singing together. The singing had a calming effect on people around us, and it became a form of sung prayer. At an especially tense moment, after our group had fallen quiet for several miles, one of the young protesters came to our group and asked us if we would please begin singing again.

At one point, we found ourselves standing toe to toe and face to face with a line of police officers in full riot gear. Here, our singing was at its most earnest and most prayerful. We could see the tension in the faces, arms, and hands of the officers before us. We were standing in the middle of a six-lane highway at 9:00 at night.

The group of protesters was eventually directed into a parking lot surrounded by a large fence on one side, the back of a store on another, and rows of hundreds of police lined up along the other two sides. More than two hundred of us were detained in this parking lot until 4:00 in the morning when we were taken to the county jail in buses. But it was during that seven hours of awaiting arrest and processing that two people from the seminaries took out a plastic bag of almonds and a water bottle. A group of us sat down in the space, surrounded by officers and other protestors, and we began to share communion. "On the night that Jesus was betrayed," a friend began. "On the night that Jesus faced the sham of a trial. On the night that Jesus lost everyone and everything, Jesus broke the bread, blessed it, and gave it to his followers." Then we shared the almonds with anyone who wanted to participate. It was the food someone had thought to bring with them that night; it became the body of Christ for us. We prayed, we gave thanks, and we even rejoiced amid the turmoil and the waiting.

On the night before he was tortured to death, Jesus knew very well that the community that had formed around him was about to be torn apart. He was aware that one of his disciples already had been so gripped by anxiety that he had betrayed Jesus to those who would soon put him to death. More than that, Jesus knew that the disintegration of his whole community was about to take place—his followers were about to abandon him and one another. In many ways, this abandonment and betrayal were inevitable, because the effects of torture in the first century were the same as they are in the twenty-first century. "Torture is the deliberate and systematic dismantling of a person's identity and humanity. Torture's purpose is to destroy a sense of community, eliminate leaders, and create a climate of fear."[15]

William Cavanaugh, in his astounding book *Torture and Eucharist*, says that the church must confront a fundamental misunderstanding about "the nature of torture as an attack on individual bodies."[16] Without doubt, torture does attack individual bodies, but individual bodies are not the primary target in the state's use of torture—the social body is.[17] Indeed, "torture is not merely an attack on, *but the creation of*, individuals."[18] Torture disintegrates community, tears people off from one another, and sets each one in an environment of distrust, anxiety, and fear. "Torture breaks down the collective links and makes of its victims isolated monads."[19] This is to the advantage of a repressive state, as Cavanaugh goes on to explain:

> Pain, as we have seen, is the great isolator, that which cuts us off in a radical way from one another. With the demolition of the victim's affective ties and loyalties, past and future, the purpose of torture is to destroy the person as a political actor, and to leave her isolated and compliant with the regime's goals. Torture is consonant with the military regime's strategy to fragment society, to disarticulate all intermediate social bodies between the individual and the state—parties, unions, professional organizations—which would challenge the regime's desire to have all depend only on it. Wherever two or three are gathered, there is subversion in their midst.[20]

It was precisely these forces that Jesus was confronting as he entered the week of his suffering. Jesus warned his disciples that they would all desert him because of what he was about to experience. He urged them to recognize that when the leader, the shepherd, is eliminated, then the community, the flock, will be scattered (Matthew 26:31). Jesus knew that the torture he would face was intended to dismantle his humanity and destroy his community.

In response, Jesus did the most remarkable thing. Before his humanity and identity could be stripped away from him at the hand of the state, Jesus *gave* himself away. "This is my body," he told his disciples, and they ate. "This is my blood," he declared to them, and they drank. In doing this, Jesus distributed himself among his followers. In eating and drinking, Jesus' followers took his identity upon themselves. No longer an individual, Jesus gave himself away to his community in such a way that the state, though they may succeed in dispersing them for a time, could not ultimately break that community apart.

If torture is a work of the state that is aimed at disintegrating and dismembering community to create radically individual bodies filled with anxiety and distrust, then how better to counter that disintegrating and dismembering force than by forming community; indeed, by *re-membering* the Body of Christ? Because simply put, to participate in community as the Body of Christ is "already to be engaged in a direct confrontation with the politics of the world."[21]

As followers of Christ, the active formation, participation, and cultivation of community is not something we get around to when we have time. It is not a luxury or an added benefit. It is not something we shrug off when we realize we don't have it. The active formation, participation, and cultivation of community is to claim *belonging* with one another. It is to see the victim of torture not with dread, but as one of us. It is to be membered together in a way that no one can tear asunder. It is to refuse anxiety as a tool of the state, and to speak freely of that which makes us fearful. It is to become a body that is empowered to speak out and act up. It is to be "a counterpower, one that unleashes worlds of life amid the deathly unmaking of worlds that war and torture spew forth."[22]

To be clear, I am not saying community is magically formed by taking communion together once a month, once a week, or even once a day. If this were the case, societal problems would have vanished millennia ago. In actuality, for many of us, communion has become solely an introspective, individual, and solitary act that just happens to occur in the middle of a bunch of people. Khalia Jelks Williams remarks, "We make a big deal of community when it comes to baptism, but when it comes to communion, it's a very individual experience. Even though we are doing it together, and we eat and drink at the same time, the language we use, and the lack of interaction, is very individually focused." Nonetheless, at its heart and from its inception, communion was intended to empower Jesus' followers to stand together, love one another, and resist together all efforts to tear their community apart.

SENDING

But the meal is not only for those gathered. As we have said before, when we eat this meal, we become it. And that meal is the Body of Christ, broken and poured out for a heart-breaking (and loved!) world. We are not fed only so that we can exist as full and satisfied fat cats. We are fed so that we can go out and do likewise. Our becoming "the body of Christ means that we then become food for the world, to be broken, given away, and consumed."[23]

The same God who sent Jesus into this world continues to send us through the power of the Holy Spirit. God's activity is always on behalf of God's creation, and we know that all of creation is groaning in anticipation of its reconciliation with God.

God draws us into the table through loving invitation. God feeds us there, nourishes us, gives us hope, and encourages us. And then we are sent away from the table. We are sent from the table into God's world. To put it another way: While we are always welcomed to the table, we are also compelled to leave it. God's missional activity is unceasing!

Liturgical scholar Ruth A. Meyers uses the image of a spinning top to convey the ways in which worship both draws us inward and then sends us outward:

> The people gather, drawn into the core of the spinning top, the heart of God's mission. Assembling as a people who have been in action in the world and carrying with them the needs and hopes of the world, the assembly offers praise, proclaims the good news of God's steadfast mercy and abiding love, and joins in the intercession of Christ. Then the assembly goes forth, the Spirit leading them out of the core of the [spinning] top into action in the world, to continue to participate in the mission of God.[24]

This movement is what Meyers refers to as missional worship—a way of understanding worship as integral to God's mission for the world. "God is a missionary God, one who calls and sends people to participate in the divine mission. From this standpoint, the church does not have a mission, but rather God's mission has a church—that is, the church serves God's mission."[25] This is why many Christians have embraced the word *missional*, because it emphasizes God's ceaseless actions to draw the world into full relationship with God. The word *missional* is intended to remind churches that it is not we who send missionaries out to some distant land to win souls; rather, we participate in God's eternal sending of God's love into the world, both near and far. "Mission is thereby seen as a movement from God to the world; the church is viewed as an instrument for that mission. There is church because there is mission, not vice versa. To participate in mission is to participate in the movement of God's love toward people, since God is a fountain of sending love."[26]

So the table around which we gather, because it is God's table, is not one where we can simply linger. It is instead a place from which we are sent to be disciples that enact God's desires for the world. Liturgical theologian Gordon Lathrop urges us to

> See to it that the holy meal is sent to those of the assembly who cannot come today, blessing the people who will carry the bread and cup to them. See to it that the collection

for the poor is given to a place or to people where it will genuinely help, especially as linked with the gifts of other assemblies. But then, follow these gifts yourselves, being staple food and festive drink for your neighbor, going to work for justice, turning again to the care for the earth.[27]

NOTES

1. Catherine Mowry LaCugna, *God for Us: The Trinity and Christian Life* (San Francisco: HarperCollins, 1993), 382.

2. That doesn't mean someone may not celebrate communion when they are alone or only with one or two other people. Every celebration of communion connects us to everyone else who has ever celebrated communion, now and in the future. The "feast" is an eschatological one that transcends time and space.

3. James E. Brenneman, "Missional Practice: A Pasadena Mennonite Church Story," in *Evangelical, Ecumenical, and Anabaptist Missiologies in Conversation*, ed. James R. Krabill, Walter Sawatsky, and Charles E. Van Engen (Maryknoll, NY: Orbis Press, 2006), 164.

4. M. Shawn Copeland, *Enfleshing Freedom: Body, Race, and Being* (Minneapolis: Fortress Press, 2009), 127–128.

5. Neil Elliot, *The People's Bible*, ed. Curtiss Paul DeYoung, Wilda C. Gafney, Leticia A. Guardiola-Sáenz, George "Tink" Tinker, and Frank M. Yamada (Minneapolis: Fortress Press, 2009), 1604.

6. Christopher J. Ellis, *Gathering: A Theology and Spirituality of Worship in Free Church Tradition* (London: SCM Press, 2004), 89–99.

7. Ellis, *Gathering*, 95.

8. See Thomas J. Talley, "History and Eschatology in the Primitive Pascha," in *Between Memory and Hope: Readings on the Liturgical Year,* ed. Maxwell E. Johnson (Collegeville, MN: The Liturgical Press, 2000), 109.

9. Orthodox theologian John D. Zizioulas calls this paradoxically "the memory of the future." Many Baptist churches that include in their communion liturgies the acclamation: "Christ has died; Christ is risen; Christ will come again!" will be able to see how it is possible to "remember" the future. As Zizioulas writes: "The Spirit is 'the Lord' who transcends linear history and turns historical continuity into a presence." See *Being as Communion* (Crestwood, NY: St Vladimir's Seminary Press, 1985), 180.

10. "We always live...between memory and hope, between his coming and his coming; and the present which is the threshold between these, between memory and hope, between past and future, this present is the locus of the presence of him who is at once Lord of history and its consummation." Talley, "History and Eschatology," 109.

11. See especially Andrea Bieler and Luise Schottroff, "Eschatological Remembrance (Anamnesis)" in *The Eucharist: Bodies, Bread, and Resurrection* (Minneapolis: Fortress Press, 2007), 157–196.

12. Bieler and Schottroff, 163.

13. Bieler and Schottroff, 166–172.

14. Ellis, *Gathering*, 121.

15. "Effects of Psychological Torture," *The Center for Victims of Torture*, https://www.cvt.org/sites/default/files/downloads/CVT%20Effects%20Torture%20April%202015.pdf. For more information about the psychological effects of torture, see the 135-page report *Break Them Down: Systemic Use of Psychological Torture*

by U.S. Forces from Physicians for Human Rights, http://physiciansforhumanrights. org/library/reports/us-torture-break-them-down-2005.html.

16. William T. Cavanaugh, *Torture and Eucharist: Theology, Politics, and the Body of Christ* (Malden, MA: Blackwell Publishing, 1998), 3.

17. Cavanaugh, 3.

18. Cavanuagh, 3.

19. Cavanaugh, 34.

20. Cavanaugh, 38.

21. Cavanaugh, 12.

22. Mark Lewis Taylor, "American Torture and the Body of Christ," in *Cross Examinations: Readings on the Meaning of the Cross Today* (Minneapolis: Augsburg Fortress Press, 2006), 276.

23. Cavanaugh, 232.

24. Ruth A. Meyers, *Missional Worship, Worshipful Mission: Gathering as God's People, Going Out in God's Name* (Grand Rapids, MI: William B. Eerdmans Publishing Co., 2014), 43.

25. Meyers, 18.

26. David J. Bosch, *Transforming Mission: Paradigm Shifts in Theology of Mission* (Maryknoll, NY: Orbis Books, 2011), 382.

27. Gordon W. Lathrop, *Holy Ground: A Liturgical Cosmology* (Minneapolis: Fortress Press, 2003), 146.

CHAPTER 9

PREPARING THE TABLE
Questions of Practice in Communion

> The truly remarkable transformation is not the one
> from unbelief to belief nor from despair to hope. The
> truly remarkable (and frightening) transformation is
> from dogma to wonder, from belief to awe.
>
> —Renita Weems[1]

EACH YEAR, AS Thanksgiving Day approaches, pretty much everywhere we turn we are reminded about the feast to come. Advertisements, magazines, school art projects, television shows, and grocery stores all feature special foods, recipes, and storylines highlighting the holiday. At my house, I'll be planning the menu, shopping for ingredients, and preparing recipes for days in advance. On the day of Thanksgiving, we often eat as lightly as we can earlier in the day, preserving our appetites for the abundant food that will be heaped on our plates later in the day. There is never any doubt that Thanksgiving is a big celebration and that it is on the horizon!

At the beginning of this book, I shared the story of my friend Claire who, despite faithfully attending worship every Sunday for sixty years, thought communion was something that got "added on" to the end of worship once a month. Her theology of communion, in other words, reflected her practice of it. In her experience, communion was mostly something supplementary to the worship service. Other parts of the service might have been shortened to accommodate the extra time needed, but everything else pretty much would stay the same. The prayers, music, Scripture, and sermon often made no reference to communion. The first mention of the ritual was at the invitation to the table when a self-contained communion liturgy was inserted into the bulletin and service—invitation, words of institution, deacons or communion ushers dispersed among the congregation with the plates of bread and juice, a communion song was sung (likely "Let Us Break Bread Together on Our Knees"), the congregation ate and drank and placed their cups in the racks on the back of the pews, and then the worship service closed as usual with a final hymn and benediction. Even if the tone of the service turns suddenly solemn, the lights are lowered, and the church organ takes on melancholy tones, when communion is simply inserted into a worship service that otherwise makes no mention of it, our experience of communion can feel cursory.

For many of us, the practice of tagging communion onto the end of the service is simply "the way we've always done it." (And what an authoritative power that phrase can take on in church life, especially when it comes to worship!) But *is* this the way we've always done it? If we trace our history back even a little further, we discover that it has not always been this way. In fact, early worship happened almost entirely around the communion table. It was from the table that prayers were led, the Scriptures were read, and the meal was eaten. Only the sermon was preached from the pulpit; everything else happened around the table.[2] Just as the kitchen table often serves as the heart of family life, so did the communion table serve as the heart of the meeting for early free-church worshipers.

If we want the communion experience to truly enrich our worship, let the whole service be about communion. From the greeting to the sending, from the singing to the praying, from the sermon to the table—pastors and worship leaders can draw the congregation's attention to the meal that will soon be set out before them. Let the anticipation for the feast of communion grow as the service moves toward that climactic moment. The greeting or call to worship can welcome people to a service where the table is at the center. The opening hymn can include a verse about communion. ("Gather Us In" by Marty Haugen includes a wonderful verse about communion and serves as an excellent opening hymn.[3]) There are numerous anthems and other choral music that focus on communion.[4] Music sung by the congregation and the choir can help set the theological context for communion and can help people have a more meaningful experience.

Prayers earlier in the service can anticipate the meal. If your congregation regularly incorporates a prayer of confession and assurance of forgiveness, you might consider shaping these prayers so that they help prepare and welcome people to the meal. Let your prayer of confession be expansive enough to include complicity with systems of injustice, and not narrowly focused on individual sins. Let your assurance of forgiveness also be an assurance of worthiness, so people know they are welcome to sit at God's table, welcome to eat the feast of grace.

Visual cues can help worshipers focus on the upcoming meal. The communion table can be lavishly set ahead of time or it can be set during the service. Members of the congregation can process in with the elements that will be blessed later—setting the table with hearty loaves and a large pitcher. The connection between the communion meal and justice can be made by inviting church members to bring up to the table canned goods for the local food bank. A prayer of blessing might be spoken not only over the communion elements but also over the food that will be sent to nourish those who are hungry. Bulletin cover art or PowerPoint® slides can feature bread and juice, wheat and grapes, or even images of feasts, celebratory meals, or soup kitchens. The use of art can help people make the connections between this symbolic meal and all meals. Art can communicate multiple, rich meanings of communion, and can be accessible to those who learn visually rather than verbally.

Let your Scripture for the day and your sermon direct people's attention to the table. If your congregation follows the Revised Common Lectionary, chances are the readings will already have something to say about communion.[5] If the pastor or your congregation chooses their own Scripture focus each week, you might select texts that highlight Jesus' table ministry, other meals throughout Scripture, or eschatological or justice-related texts where eating together can give us a glimpse into God's vision for the world.

Finally, when you send people out at the close of the service, help them see that their sending is a part of the meal itself. We are sent precisely because we have been gathered at God's table. We have eaten because God desires us to feed others. We have received because God desires us to give away. We have become the Body of Christ so that we might go into the world and recognize Christ in the least of these.

IS COMMUNION ONLY FOR BAPTIZED BELIEVERS?

One thing leads to another. Traditionally, that has been the most accurate way to describe the relationship between baptism and communion, and the reason many churches have held that only baptized believers should take communion. As early as the late fourth century, it was common for catechists (those preparing for the rite of baptism) to be excused from worship at the point when the community began to celebrate communion. While the rest of the congregation shared the bread and cup, those preparing for baptism would be in classes to learn about what it means to become a follower of Jesus.[6] These classes would usually happen during what would become the season of Lent, with baptisms occurring during the Easter celebration. Connecting baptism with the celebration of Easter made a strong connection between baptism and Jesus' death and resurrection. After the baptisms, worship would conclude with communion—and those who had been newly baptized would receive communion for the first time as full members of the Body of Christ.[7]

Historically, Baptists have grappled with the question of how closed or open the communion meal should be. Some Baptists limited communion to members of the congregation only, some limited it to only those who had only been baptized by immersion, some opened it to those who had been baptized in any form (including those who were baptized as infants).[8] Some churches allowed baptized members of other congregations to receive communion only after they had received a letter of recommendation from their home church.[9] Whether open or closed, admission to the table was at a minimum reliant on baptism.

In early American free-church worship, church members were sometimes excluded from receiving communion as a result of church discipline. (This refusal to offer communion is the technical definition of *excommunication*.[10]) Generally, proceedings for church discipline would occur during midweek and afternoon worship, when a church member would be cleared of charges or given opportunity to repent. In the absence of contrition, a member would be excommunicated usually for a brief period, perhaps four weeks or six months, but sometimes longer. Reasons for excommunication tended to be focused on behavior that affected the health of the community and family relationships. The offenses included lying, stealing, adultery, child abuse, abuse of servants, unethical business practices, bringing false charges against others, and more.[11] The excommunicated member was permitted to attend worship, but not to receive the bread or wine.[12] They also would lose their right to vote in congregational meetings.[13] Church members were not allowed to socialize or share any meals with the excommunicated member; although family members were permitted to continue to share meals at home with her or him.[14] To be readmitted to communion, the disciplined member would have to undergo the same process as a new, prospective member would. After this, their full participation in community life was restored.

Churches today face the challenge of weighing these historical precedents against their theological commitments when it comes to their decision as to whether to practice closed or open communion.[15] But if the question is framed in terms of which practice is most reflective of Jesus' ministry and his proclamation of good news, then our best practice is to provide an open table. As we saw in chapters seven and eight, the accounts of Jesus' table fellowship as well as his healing ministry consistently reveal his concern to end segregation, disrupt understandings of holiness and purity, and seek to bring those at the margins into the center of community.[16] In his Parable of the Wedding Banquet, Jesus makes it plain: "When you give a luncheon or a dinner, do not invite your friends or your brothers or your relatives or rich neighbors, in case they may invite you in return, and you would be repaid. But when you give a banquet, invite the poor, the crippled, the lame, and the blind" (Luke 14:12-13).

According to church historian Susan Wessel, for early Christians "the table was a complex metaphor for the power relations implied by social interaction. It was also a metaphor for the eschatological reversal implied by the ritual meal Jesus shared with his followers."[17] Then, as now, the open table becomes a word of judgment and grace. The table is a word of judgment, because it exposes our human attempts to establish hard-and-fast categories of who is in and who is out. As Khalia Jelks Williams puts it, it is at the divine table that "God allows us to see who we are for who we really are." Yet the table also speaks a message of grace, because it reveals God's extravagant, prodigal love for the world and all its inhabitants. God's invitation is extended to all, every seeking soul in every condition, in every place, and for all time.

God poured out God's love for the world without asking that the world be worthy of this extravagance (Romans 5:1-10). Because we are recipients of this astounding grace, we must also cooperate with God's desire to extend that grace to all. "Having been embraced by God, we must make space for others in ourselves and invite them in—even our enemies."[18] For Debora Jackson, the realization that the table needed to remain open came gently to her over time as she pastored. "It doesn't matter if you belonged to the church. It doesn't matter if you haven't been baptized. The grace of God is given us freely. I don't have to ask for it. I don't have to be in right relationship. It was given to me before I even knew who God was. And so how would I deny someone else an act which I think is part of the grace of God?"

Don Ng explains: "We are all connected. If we can begin to understand what that means through our celebration of the Lord's Supper, then we will be led to believe that every person is a brother or sister, that every person belongs to the family of God. So, these tribes we talk about? It's really one tribe, one human race."

SHOULD CHILDREN RECEIVE COMMUNION?

I'll never forget the Sunday in worship when I passed the plate of bread over the head of my two-year-old son who was seated beside me. He looked up at me in confusion as I held a piece of bread in my hand. "I'm hungry, too," he told me. My heart broke. And in my spirit, I heard the echo of Jesus' question: "Is there any among you who, if your child asks for bread, will give a stone?" (Matthew 7:9).

Because our churches practice believers' baptism, the question of how best to incorporate children into the life of the congregation can be especially fraught. We want to affirm the growing faith of the children in our congregation, want them to feel fully a part of the community, while also providing the space they need to come to their own decisions of faith. Debora Jackson remembers, "Growing up in the Black Baptist church, you couldn't take communion if you hadn't been baptized. The elements passed you by. And it was something I remembered as a child, watching and not quite understanding why I could not participate. Probably one of the motivating factors of my being baptized as young as I was—I was baptized at ten—was because I wanted to be part of the community. I wanted to take part in communion." Her exclusion from communion as a young child instilled in Debora a desire for full belonging that ended up playing an important role in her decision to follow Christ. Nonetheless, as we see above, Debora feels it is important to provide a table open to all, including children.

James Brenneman encourages churches to welcome children at the table "because the Passover meal upon which it is modeled was always open to children."[19] The Passover Seder is actually geared toward children. "Its primary purpose was educational and invitational to begin the incorporation of children into the salvation history of the people of God at the level of their understanding."[20] Brenneman describes the Lord's Supper as a mnemonic device, "a meal of memory, a gift passed along of profound identity and blessing to our children preparing them for the time when they will appropriate this belief by a more mature self-conscious decision followed by baptism."[21]

Indeed, as my son reminded me so simply and profoundly, children are hungry, too. By gifting our communities with a supper at the heart of our shared life together, Jesus helps us remember that hunger is always both about our bodies and about more than our bodies. "When one is hungry, it is not just a personal and physical matter; it also becomes a spiritual, theological, and public issue," writes HyeRan Kim-Cragg, professor of pastoral studies at St. Andrew's College at the University of Saskatchewan.[22] Allowing our children to eat at the table with us, we offer them a food that can sustain them beyond what they can understand in the moment. Likewise, Brenneman writes:

> Before a watching world hungry for table fellowship, starving for authentic relationships, eager to learn about God's saving purposes, an open, inviting, Holy Communion that includes children reminds us all of the process leading to salvation: "Let the little children come to me, and do not hinder them, for the kingdom of God belongs to such as these. I tell you the truth: anyone who does not receive the kingdom of God like a little child will never enter it" (Mark 10:14-16).[23]

WHO CAN PRESIDE?

There is no hard-and-fast rule about who can and cannot preside at the table, although the practice in any particular congregation may feel ironclad! In considering this question (and others surrounding leadership in worship), one helpful exercise is to ask churchgoers to identify the holiest or most sacred places in the sanctuary. You'll likely get a variety of answers, and each one could be fruitful to explore! But among the top answers will likely be the pulpit, the chancel (or "stage" as some free-church folks might say), and the communion table. Once the most sacred sites are identified, next ask, Who gets to stand in those places? Who is visible? Who has the privilege to be closest to the most sacred places in the church? Is it only people who have been ordained? Is it only men? Is it only adults? Is it only those who are able-bodied? Then ask yourselves if this is the message your church intends to convey in its worship week after week, month after month, and year after year.

Who we see occupying the most sacred and important places shapes our theologies. It shapes our understanding of who is most valued and heard. It shapes our vision of what is possible or what is not possible. Sometimes we don't realize how much this is true until we try something different in worship. When recollecting an especially meaningful communion experience, Khalia Jelks Williams recalled the time her husband, Damon Williams, senior pastor of the historical Providence Missionary Baptist Church in Atlanta, GA, invited two children to preside at the communion table with him. Before the service began, he walked them through what they would do and gave them a brief explanation of what happens at the table. Khalia says that when the time for communion came, "he asked all the children to stand. He talked about what it means that Christ invites us to the table, talked about the symbol of Christ's broken body, and the symbol of Christ's shed blood, and why we do what we do. It was a truly elementary explanation, and it was so clear," Khalia remembered. "Then seeing the nine-year-old sister breaking the bread, and her eleven-year-old brother picking up the pitcher and pouring the juice into the chalice? Seeing them become real leaders at that table, because they were the ones who were presenting the elements of communion to the congregation? That stood out. I didn't gauge the impact it would have on me. That was a wow-moment for me. It was breathtaking. And really humbling to realize that this is how we should come to the table every time, with hearts as kids."

Having children assist in leadership at the communion table opened the congregation to the realization that someone does not need to be ordained clergy to handle the bread and cup. Since that Sunday, Pastor Williams has had deaconesses preside with him. "That has become such a great picture for me," Khalia shared. "To see a 38-year-old pastor and a 78-year-old deaconess, standing together, leading at the table together? It is so good to see. It really is."

"I remember years ago when a group of us at Grace Baptist Church in Chicago had a rule in communion that there could not be only one gender officiating at the table. There had to be both genders present," Tim Phillips, pastor of Seattle First Baptist, told me one afternoon. "Then some years later, we visited another church out in California, and it was communion Sunday. Only the pastor, who was a man, was presiding at the table. I turned to my partner at the time and I said, 'Does this feel strange to you?' And he said, 'Yes, what is it?' And I said, 'Well, we don't do communion anymore where there is only a man serving communion at the table.' It had been so long since we had seen this that it seemed shocking in a way. At Seattle First Baptist we never have just one person at the table. And now, of course, we have to think beyond just male and female."

By intentionally paying attention to who stands at the table, we can positively shape theologies that allow us to see God's presence in many different bodies—differently gendered, differently aged, differently abled, differently educated, differently sized, and on and on.

FREQUENCY OF COMMUNION

Most Baptist congregations celebrate communion twelve times a year—that is, once a month on the first Sunday of the month. Some will include communion as part of a special service on Maundy Thursday. But the sense for many free-church folks is that too frequent celebration of communion would make the experience routine and less meaningful. Celebrating the Lord's Supper only once a month is intended to highlight its elevated status. But as we have discussed, whether this is how people interpret their experience remains a question.

When considering the frequency of communion, I think it's important for Baptists to remember that *we are a free-church worshiping tradition.* That means there is nothing in our church polity and no denominational expectation that we must celebrate communion once a month and only once a month. We have the freedom to gather for communion more often if we feel led to do so. And, while it may seem somewhat contrary to other things we have said here, we can also celebrate communion less frequently, if it should make sense for us to do so.

While I was attending a Lutheran seminary, I had the opportunity to attend the seminary's weekly communion service at chapel every Wednesday. For me, the experience of receiving communion once a week was deeply meaningful. I found that it heightened my sense of my need for God's nourishment, and it led me to appreciate the symbolic re-formation of the Body of Christ. I found that approaching the communion table with my hands empty and open, week after week, allowed my spirit to remain open to God's presence in a deeply life-giving way through the rest of the week. Receiving communion regularly amid the weekly ups and downs and the regular rhythm of life made communion *more relevant* to my life, not more routine. During those years, if I missed communion for any reason, I felt the loss of it. I looked forward to the next time we would gather with a feeling of even greater need. As a spiritual practice, weekly communion fed me, challenged me, and helped me know God's grace.

Congregations that want to explore more deeply the meaning of communion may want to decide to try celebrating communion more often, at least for a season. This is where our freedom to make our own choices in worship can be exercised! If your congregation is studying this book right now, for example, you may want to try a six-week worship series in which you celebrate communion every week. Allow the whole worship service to focus on communion themes; craft sermons that draw people's attention to the communion meal, to Jesus' other meals, and to justice themes related to food production, food sharing, and God's vision for the world; sing songs that celebrate the communion meal and speak to eschatological images of feasting. Let the congregation experience a weekly rhythm of eating together and help people anticipate that God can show up for us at the meal week after week without our losing track of how astoundingly grace-filled that is.

What I most want you to understand is that you can do this *temporarily*, in the same way that you might choose to focus a series of weekly sermons on the parables of Jesus or the Beatitudes. Deciding to share communion more frequently for a few weeks does not mean you are committing to a weekly celebration forever.

You may also decide to find ways to celebrate communion more frequently without altering the monthly rhythm of the Sunday worship experience. Consider other opportunities when the congregation or groups within it might share communion together. These can be at church retreats, at youth group, or as a part of Wednesday night suppers during the season of Lent. You can also provide a liturgy for families to follow at home, should they wish to celebrate communion as a part of their own devotional practice.

At the same time, know that you may also decide not to share communion together one month. Nearly thirty years ago, when I was part of a worship planning team at Central Baptist Church in Wayne, Pennsylvania, we created a worship series for the season of Lent that focused on Jesus' time in the wilderness when he fasted for forty days. As part of our series, we were focusing on a sense of lament, naming before God the broken and desolate places in the world and our lives. The first Sunday of a month fell early in that season, and we felt a celebration of communion would work against the sense of wilderness time that we had chosen to enter. We decided we would fast from communion that month, allowing its absence to speak deeply to us. It was a risky thing to try! People came to worship expecting to receive communion. We felt its loss! I can also assure you that when we returned to the table the following month, the communion meal felt like a feast indeed! After our time of wilderness, communion became our oasis. There was great celebration that we could gather once again at this grace-filled supper.

Ultimately, as with all things for those of us in free-church traditions, it is up to each congregation to make its own decision about frequency of communion. We can make our decisions most responsibly by making it intentionally and by regularly revisiting the decision. Understand why we tend to celebrate only once a month. Do not choose to celebrate communion more often only because that's how our more liturgical sisters and brothers do it. Make a decision that is rooted in robust theological reflection. Involve a cross-section of the congregation in the decision. Be open to experimentation. And seek to do well whatever you decide to do. Craft services that are meaningful and rich, whether they only happen twelve times a year, or if they happen fifty-two times a year.

ON EATING LOCALLY AND FOOD ALLERGIES

Until I began interviewing people for this book, I never knew there were so many people who associated Pepperidge Farms® white bread (the crusts carefully cut off, of course) with the bread of Holy Communion! James White reminds us that the everyday quality of foods like this is an important part of what communion means. "The use of common food is at the heart of the eucharist. Christ did not choose nectar and ambrosia, the food of the gods, but bread and wine, the food of humans."[24] The use of common (and recognizable!) bread at the communion table can help us remember that while this meal is special, it is also ordinary. Indeed, we worship a God who can be known, indeed desires to be known, by us in everyday, ordinary moments.

We would do well, however, to raise questions about the economic implications of buying name-brand, global, processed food to serve at the communion table. We need to consider the labor that produced that food, the profit that is drawn from selling it, and the chemicals that might be added to preserve it. Reflecting on corporate food production, HyeRan Kim-Cragg notes, "It is ironic to note that the bread signifying the Reign of God is manufactured by a profit-driven industry symbolic of global capitalism that benefits a few rather than being shared by all."[25] Simply serving food as communion does not transform its production into something just. Even the communion table can be complicit in unjust systems.

While it's likely impossible to provide "pure" food and drink with every ingredient responsibly and sustainably produced, we can do more to limit the damage. Invite members of the congregation to bake bread for communion each month. Some Sunday school classes have children prepare the bread, and the smell of it wafts throughout the church. Use local bakeries or food co-ops to provide communion bread. Try to buy grape juice or wine that is produced locally or sustainably.

When considering food allergies, Joe Kutter notes, "Things are a lot more complicated today than they used to be. If I were still a pastor today," he continues, "I would have to talk to the congregation asking, 'What works here, and what are the issues?' And I would make absolutely certain that parents 35 and younger were a part of the conversation. Because we didn't have the concern about food allergies 70 years ago. You just did what you did. But you can't do that anymore. So make sure that conversation is alive and well and *ongoing*."

While the Vatican prohibits the use of gluten-free bread in communion, free churches have much more leeway when it comes to what is served at the table.[26] Congregations need to be aware that a table with only traditional bread is not welcoming for those who live with celiac disease, an immune disorder triggered by gluten that causes stomach pain, diarrhea and weight loss, but has also been linked to depression, infertility, arthritis, and anemia. Others with allergies or sensitivities to gluten suffer some of these symptoms as well. For some with celiac disease, even being in a space where gluten is present can trigger serious reactions. Serving gluten-free options alongside regular bread, or handling bread with gluten, then handling gluten-free bread will still cause contamination. Therefore, if you are hoping to be accommodating for everyone, it is best to only serve gluten-free bread rather than making both options available. Including a word in the bulletin about the bread being gluten-free will alert visitors with celiac disease that they are welcome to receive communion. Likewise, if you are not serving gluten-free bread, it is helpful to make note of that in the bulletin or in pre-service announcements as well.

GRAPE JUICE OR (GASP!) WINE?

Tony Campolo, in his inimitable style, has been known to quip, "Different denominations approach communion differently. Catholics believe that the bread and wine literally become the body and blood of Jesus; Lutherans believe that the bread stays bread and the wine stays wine, but that Christ is still present in them; I'm a Baptist and we believe that the bread stays bread and the wine becomes grape juice."[27] The common practice of serving grape juice at communion is only about a hundred years old. With its roots in the temperance movement in the United States, serving grape juice, and specifically Welch's grape juice, seemed a natural choice for denominations that forbade the use of alcohol.[28]

As it happens, serving grape juice at communion does make communion a more broadly welcoming practice. It allows those who struggle with alcohol dependency or alcoholism to drink from the cup along with everyone else. (In congregations that only serve wine, those who are unable to receive the cup will cross their arms and receive a spoken blessing, or they will kiss the cup rather than drink from it.) In its circular letter that prohibited the use of gluten-free bread in communion, the Vatican did allow for the use of *mustum*, a grape juice where fermentation is stopped almost immediately so there is less than 1 percent alcohol content. But even in this case, many people would prefer to abstain from drinking it.

Now that serving grape juice is such a dominant practice among Baptists, it might seem downright scandalous to suggest that a Baptist church could serve wine at communion. But just like everything else in worship, it is important for us to know the history of how things came to be the way they are. And we are, especially as free-church folks, more than able to question whether the practices we do today reflect our present commitments. If they do, then we can continue following them; if they don't, we can change. The decision to change should follow a careful process, with as much of the congregation's participation as possible. And the conversation should be ongoing. I have been a part of a Baptist congregation that chose to serve wine at communion only for our Ash Wednesday services. Even then, both wine and grape juice were served, so congregants could decide from which cup they would drink.[29]

INCULTURATION

It is essential to point out that these questions of bread, grape juice, and wine are culturally bound. These are foods that are readily available only in certain parts of the world, and they are definitely not common in all parts of the world where we find Christians practicing communion! If it is the ordinary nature of the food Jesus presented at the Last Supper that we wish to emphasize, then we need to recognize that bread and grape juice are not ordinary food for much of the world. Russell Yee writes, "The ultimate goal, it seems to me, is simply to get us to eat and drink together in Jesus' name as an act of worship in which we are nourished by his very life. Beyond that, we have wide freedom about the particular foodstuffs used and the particular qualities they convey."[30]

HyeRan Kim-Cragg advocates that we dive into Scripture and early church practices to discover the diverse and rich variety of foods that could be served at communion:

For far too long we have assumed a uniformity of Eucharistic practice without sufficient theological reason. We must get away from using one kind of food in the Eucharist, by drinking from the biblical and theological well of wisdom. The food and the drink that early Christians used were diverse, localized, and pluriform. Indeed, the Eucharist involved the sharing of fruits, vegetables, and fish instead of strictly using bread. Other liquids such as water, milk, and oil were also used instead of wine. Early Christian novels depict Eucharistic meals without wine but with vegetables.[31]

Such a delicious listing of food and drink helps us perceive the intended connections between the symbolic meal of communion, and the everyday meals that nourish our bodies, our spirits, our minds, and our communities.

For congregations in parts of the world where bread and wine or grape juice are not ordinary foods, and for some congregations in the United States, there is a strong precedent for using the food and drink that is most common in their own cultures. Russell Yee relates a story of a communion service in a Japanese American congregation where they served senbei crackers and hot green tea. At the table, Yee recalls, the presider explained, "We usually use grape juice because of its color—it's dark like blood. But today I'm using tea, *which is warm—like blood.*" Yee goes on to reflect, "It was a startling and moving breakthrough moment in which an ANA [Asian North American] staple—hot tea—conveyed something true and freshly remembered about Jesus' self-sacrifice."[32] The use of tea, kava, or goat milk, and the use of rice, pita, or fish are possible ways to invite people to share a communion meal with rich significance.

JUNK FOOD AND COMMUNION

A friend told me recently about an especially meaningful communion experience she had some years ago. "But it wasn't your usual communion," she told me.[33] It was after a weekend of committee meetings for a church-related group. The meetings had been very contentious, with difficult decisions and some brokenness in relationships. While the group knew they would have a closing worship service, they hadn't planned on serving communion. Then late Saturday night someone suggested that sharing communion might help heal some of the brokenness they had experienced together. Without the ability to get to a grocery store, the group scrounged around the conference center for something that could stand in for the communion elements. Someone found a can of lemonade, and someone else some Saltine crackers. It was close enough, they felt. It would have to do. "I was surprised," my friend told me. "Somehow or other, it worked." The use of these unusual ingredients for communion, especially the shock of tasting the bittersweet lemonade, seemed to wake them up to a deeper experience of this otherwise familiar rite. "It was an acknowledgment of all that was bitter, and a hope that something good could come out of it." she reflected. "Of course, not everything was magically fixed after that. But I always felt that communion service was the first baby step in our healing process."

Like the few fragments of bread and couple of fish in John's Gospel, God turned what could be found into a small meal that would somehow nourish for years to come. The lemonade wasn't used because someone thought it would be cute, edgy, or clever. It was chosen because that was what they could find. And as God does all the time, God used the ordinary to reveal something extraordinary.

No food is too lowly, no moment too ordinary, that God's presence cannot be known in it. The question isn't whether God can make use of empty-calorie food and drink used as symbols for Christ's body and blood. Rather, we need to ask ourselves what theological and ethical meanings get conveyed by the food we serve as part of communion. It is best if our symbols can be robust. Even as a symbolic meal, the food and drink that is served at communion ought to be real food whenever that is possible. We ought to know that what we are eating and drinking can sustain us.

RETREATS AND YOUTH GROUP

When seminary students begin to learn more about the theology and meaning of worship, they sometimes start to feel a little frustrated at how difficult it can be to introduce new ways of doing things in churches. In studying this book, you may feel a little bit of that same frustration. Communion may be done a particular way in your church, and there may be very little possibility of ever trying anything too different on a Sunday morning. But even if you are a part of a worshiping community that *doesn't* mind trying new things, I encourage you to see retreats and youth group events as opportunities to try new things with less fear of upsetting people.

Communion can happen in the church fellowship hall, or the youth group basement, or under the redwoods, or at the beach. All of these can be very meaningful, significant, and memorable experiences for people. These special occasions can let people try something new without feeling all the weight of a traditional worship service upon them. In these alternate settings, people might be more willing to try serving one another communion, doing communion by intinction (dipping the bread into the juice), letting youth say the blessing over the bread and cup, or sharing communion in small groups, or at worship stations set around the room. These unthreatening situations can open people up to deeper meanings and experiences of communion, which, slowly and over time, may gently allow a congregation to try new practices in Sunday morning worship as well.

WORLD COMMUNION SUNDAY

World Communion Sunday, originally called World Wide Communion Sunday, began in the Presbyterian Church (USA) in 1936. Always intended to be an ecumenical celebration, the organization that would become the National Council of Churches of Christ embraced World Communion Sunday in 1940. The practice continues today in many churches around the world. Celebrated on the first Sunday of October, World

Communion Sunday is intended to make Christians around the globe more aware of our connections with one another. Some churches use this occasion to intentionally include different languages in their worship service, or invite church members to set out different breads or food from around the world to be shared at the communion table that day.

Edward Phillips raises some critical questions about the practice of providing an assortment of breads at communion on World Communion Sunday, worrying that it turns communion into "an object lesson about the multicultural span of the church," results in too many leftovers, and "mimics a food mart at the local mall that offers a choice of ethnic cuisines without genuine cultural context."[34] Some of Phillips's concerns can be alleviated by inviting members of the congregation to bring breads and other food that is representative of their own cultures. Those who bring food for the table that Sunday might also be given the opportunity to share something of significance about what that bread or food means for them culturally. A litany that incorporates mention of the breads and cultures represented might also make the event more meaningful and less like a food court. Be careful, of course, not to essentialize the various cultures mentioned. Prayers that focus on different parts of the world can also be especially meaningful on this day. If your church sponsors missionaries, World Communion Sunday would be a good occasion to pray for your missionaries by name. And don't forget that other churches in your neighborhood or city are included in this world! Perhaps this would be a wonderful day to reach out to neighboring churches and do an exchange—invite some members to worship with you and send some of your members to worship elsewhere.

World Communion Sunday can be a great practice, especially for churches that have a congregational polity. It is very helpful for us all to remember that we really are connected to Christians around the globe; including Christians with worshiping traditions very different from our own. It is equally important to remember, though, that every Sunday that we share communion, we are doing so in the company of Christians around the world (and right next door). Remember other churches and communities in your prayers whenever you gather, and especially on communion Sundays.

NOTES

1. Renita Weems, *Listening for God: A Minister's Journey Through Silence and Doubt* (New York: Touchstone, 1999), 187–188.

2. Doug Adams, *Meeting House to Camp Meeting: Toward a History of American Free Church Worship from 1620 to 1835* (Saratoga, NY and Austin, TX: Modern Liturgy-Resource Publications and The Sharing Company, 1981), 13.

3. Text and music by Marty Haugen, 1979. Text and music © 1982 GIA Publications, Inc. Search https:/hymnary.org/ to find hymns that focus on communion.

4. SongSelect, a service of Christian Copyright Licensing International, is a great place to find worship music for purposeful worship planning. Their service allows you to print needed lyrics, choral, lead, and vocal sheets while also following copyright laws. See https://us.ccli.com for more information. One License also provides similar services at https://www.onelicense.net/. Explore each of these sites to find the one that would most suit your congregation's needs.

5. Because the Revised Common Lectionary was based initially on the Lectionary for Mass from the Roman Catholic tradition, many of the Sunday lectionary texts had a eucharistic focus. For more information on how the Revised Common Lectionary was shaped, see Fritz West, *Scripture and Memory: The Ecumenical Heritage of the Three-Year Lectionaries* (Collegeville, MN: The Liturgical Press, 1997).

6. Note that catechists learned about what it means to be a follower of Jesus in their baptism classes. They didn't learn what *baptism* meant. It was only after they experienced baptism that the initiates would then have classes to reflect on the meanings of baptism, communion, and other sacraments. These latter teachings were known as *mystagogy*. See Enrico Mazza, *Mystagogy: A Theology of Liturgy in the Patristic Age* (Collegeville, MN: The Liturgical Press, 1989).

7. It is important to understand that just like today, there were tremendously diverse and varied practices in the early churches. For a more in-depth description of the origins of baptism in multiple contexts, see Maxwell E. Johnson, *The Rites of Christian Initiation: Their Evolution and Interpretation* (Collegeville, MN: The Liturgical Press, 1999).

8. See Bill J. Leonard, *Baptist Ways: A History* (Valley Forge, PA: Judson Press, 2003).

9. Leonard, 50.

10. A lighter sentence would be to admonish someone. Admonishment also resulted in a member not being allowed to receive communion for a short time, but their membership in the community was not revoked. See Adams, *Meeting House to Camp Meeting*, 50–51.

11. See Adams, 40–55.

12. Adams, 51.

13. Adams, 51.

14. Adams, 51.

15. Some churches may be surprised to discover that whether their communion practice is closed or open is written into their bylaws. Some congregations might be aware of the stated position in their bylaws yet choose to ignore it. Others might decide that it is important to go through a process of revising their bylaws to reflect current theological commitments.

16. For more on this, see Peniel Rajkumar, *Dalit Theology and Dalit Liberation: Problems, Paradigms, and Possibilities* (New York, Routledge Press, 2016);

George M. Soares-Prabhu, "The Table Fellowship of Jesus: Its Significance for Dalit Christians in India Today," in *The Dharma of Jesus*, ed. Francis Xavier D'sa (Maryknoll, NY: Orbis, 2003), 117–132; Marcus J. Borg, *Conflict, Holiness, and Politics in the Teachings of Jesus* (New York: Continuum, 1998).

17. Susan Wessel, *Passion and Compassion in Early Christianity* (New York: Cambridge University Press, 2016), 76.

18. Miroslav Volf, *Exclusion and Embrace: A Theological Exploration of Identity, Otherness, and Reconciliation* (Nashville: Abingdon Press, 1996), 129.

19. James E. Brenneman, "Missional Practice: A Pasadena Mennonite Church Story," in *Evangelical, Ecumenical, and Anabaptist Missiologies in Conversation*, ed. James R. Krabill, Walter Sawatsky, and Charles E. Van Engen (Maryknoll, NY: Orbis Press, 2006), 162.

20. Brenneman, 162.

21. Brenneman, 163.

22. HyeRan Kim-Cragg, "Through Senses and Sharing: How Liturgy Meets Food," *Liturgy* 32:2 (2017): 39. http://dx.doi.org/10.1080/0458063X.2017.1262642.

23. Brenneman, 163.

24. James F. White, *Introduction to Christian Worship*, 3rd ed. (Nashville: Abingdon Press, 2000), 261.

25. Kim-Cragg, 37.

26. Congregation for Divine Worship and the Discipline of the Sacraments, "Circular letter to Bishops on the bread and wine for the Eucharist," Prot. N. 320/17 http://www.vatican.va/roman_curia/congregations/ccdds/documents/rc_con_ccdds_doc_20170615_lettera-su-pane-vino-eucaristia_en.html.

27. Tony Campolo, cited in Drew McIntyre, "'To Wonder and Adore': Recovering Communion as Holy Mystery," Via Media Methodists, https://viamedia methodists.wordpress.com/2015/09/03/to-wonder-adore-recovering-communion-as-holy-mystery/.

28. For an excellent account of how Welch's grape juice came to be dominant in North American Protestant churches, see Russell Yee, *Worship on the Way: Exploring Asian North American Christian Experience* (Valley Forge, PA: Judson Press, 2012), 138–139.

29. While the theological significance of one cup is strong, practically it is more welcoming to offer both grape juice and wine, if a congregation decides to provide wine at the table. In this case, it would need to be unmistakably clear which cup had the wine and which cup the grape juice, so no one receives wine unaware. Of course, since the early twentieth century, it has been common practice to serve grape juice in individual cups, which only further blurs the symbolism of sharing a common cup.

30. Yee, 143.

31. Kim-Cragg, 37.

32. Yee, 143.

33. Names and details have been changed in this story.

34. Edward Phillips, "Eucharist and the Meaning of Ordinary Food," *Liturgy* 32:2, (2017): 32, http://dx.doi.org/10.1080/045806X.2017.1262640.

CHAPTER **10**

WORSHIP RESOURCES FOR SERVICES OF COMMUNION

Table Prayer

SHARON R. FENNEMA

This table prayer imagines members of a community seated around tables to celebrate communion, with two or more people serving as leaders. The instructions/prompts in italics could be printed on cards and placed on the tables, included in the bulletin, or projected if desired. This prayer could also be used in the context of an agape *meal or a community potluck.*

Invitation—Centering Meditation

LEADER 1: As we come together around these tables for a meal,
much like we might any other day,
we do so knowing how permeable they are,
how, in the space of a breath,
they can become all we know of grace and hope,
compassion and justice.

So as we come together around these tables for this holy meal,
much like we might any other day,
you are invited to take a moment to center yourself,
to breathe in the smell of the food...
to breathe with those gathered at table with you...
to close your eyes or let them find a soft focus...
and imagine in the silence of your heart...
What does the Holy taste like?

Does it taste like the sweet refreshment of a popsicle on a hot summer afternoon?

Does it taste like the savory comfort of *chile rellenos,*
bursting with warm melty *queso?*
Does it taste like the jammy tenderness of a peanut
   butter and jelly sandwich,
given to you when the cupboards are bare?
Does it taste like the basic ordinariness of bread?

What does the Holy taste like?

Beloved ones, this sweet and savory Holy One
draws us together and welcomes us here,
inviting us to make each table and each meal a place
where we taste and see the goodness of our God.

Table Prayer

LEADER 1: As a people loved and welcomed, challenged and
   delighted in,
as the priesthood of all believers,
let us, together, create and pray our table prayer.

LEADER 2: We give you thanks, Holy One, our Creator,
for the beauty and mystery of your creation,
Through this creation, you teach us to wonder and
   delight
at the many ways your imaginative love is made
   manifest in the world.

LEADER 3: Share with those at your table a word or short phrase
   of gratitude for God's love made known to us in
   creation.
For what are you grateful?...

LEADER 1: We give you thanks, Holy One our Redeemer,
for the good news of your life and ministry, death and
   resurrection.
Through this salvation, you show us the ways of
   resilience and resistance in the face of injustice,
   compassion and mercy in the face of suffering.

LEADER 2: Share with those at your table a word or short phrase of
   lament for the life-limiting, death-dealing ways of our
   world.
What do you lament?...

LEADER 3: We give you thanks, Holy One our Sustainer,
for your continued work among us.
Through this inspiration, you empower us
to give voice to our deepest longings

and order our steps in the ways of justice and peace.

LEADER 1: Share with those at your table a word or short phrase of witness to the prophetic moving of the Spirit.
Where do you find hope?...

LEADER 2: Overflowing with gratitude, we join our hearts in prayer and praise with those who have gone before us. We hold space for the chairs at the table which remain empty, knowing that with you, absence is also always presence...

LEADER 3: Say to those at your table the name of one ancestor in faith, one saint who gathers with you there.
Who do you remember?

LEADER 1: With these beloved ancestors and all creation
we praise you, Gracious God, who is love in community,
that our stories take place within your story,
that each and every meal can be a revelation of your presence among us,
a celebration of the communion we share with you and each other,
a foretaste of the feast of justice and joy that is to come.
We celebrate the echoes of your last meal in this meal we share as we remember.

LEADER 2: Remember the narrative with one another,
each contributing a part to the telling,
You know the story; say the words to each other.
On the night in which Jesus was betrayed...

[At this point members of the community are invited to say to one another some form of the Words of Institution. Alternatively, a minister could say those words/offer that prayer here.]

LEADER 3: Would someone at each table take the bread and break it?

LEADER 1: We break this bread remembering the brokenness of our world and declaring that our hope of wholeness and shalom is in Christ.

LEADER 2: Would someone at each table take the cup and raise it?

LEADER 3: We hold this cup remembering the pain and bloodshed of our world
and declaring our hope in the overflowing love of Christ.

LEADER 1: Let us all extend our hands over the bread and cups, as you are willing and able.

LEADER 2: As we have poured out our gratitude, so now, Gracious God,
pour out your Holy Spirit among us,
blessing this bread and cup, and all who share in it with your peace and power.
As the bread and cup which we now eat and drink are changed into us,
transform us so that we might change the world.
In the name of all that is Holy, Just, and Compassionate, we pray. Amen.

LEADER 3: This is the feast of God's love. Let us taste and see the goodness of our God.

LEADER 1: Eat, drink, and make glad!

Remember Me: The Intinction of Bread into Water
Communion Liturgy to Remember the Prisoners
JEAN JEFFRESS

LEADER 1: Jesus said when you take the bread and the cup, remember me.

ALL: Remember me.

LEADER 2: When we remember, we add again something or someone to our lives that was lost or forgotten. We re-member something to our world.

ALL: Remember me.

LEADER 1: Remembering can be co-opted by powers and principalities by the tucking away of certain facts and figures, the rewriting of history to disappear certain events and people from the passage of time.

ALL: Remember me.

LEADER 2: Jesus said, "For I was hungry and you gave me food, I was thirsty and you gave me something to drink, I was a stranger and you welcomed me, I was naked and you gave me clothing, I was sick and you took care of me, I was in prison and you visited me."

LEADER 1: Then the righteous will answer him, "Lord, when was it that we saw you hungry and gave you food, or thirsty and gave you something to drink? And when was it that we saw you a stranger and welcomed you, or naked and gave you clothing? And when was it that we saw you sick or in prison and visited you?"

LEADER 2: "Truly I tell you, just as you did it to one of the least of these who are members of my family, you did it to me."

ALL: Remember me.

LEADER 2: Today we remember Jesus through the least of these. We lift bread and cup and open our hearts to remember, to add again to our consciousness, and to our field of vision, the 2.4 million human beings who are incarcerated in the United States. We remember you.

ALL: Remember me.

LEADER 1: We lift bread and cup and remember the prisoners on labor and hunger strikes right now in prisons all across the country refusing to work as slave labor for corporations who profit off human misery. We remember you.

ALL: Remember me.

LEADER 2: We lift bread and cup and remember the prisoners in solitary confinement, people who are tucked away, disappeared, whose lives are trying to be written out of the passage of time by the hand of oppression. We remember you.

ALL: Remember me.

LEADER 1: We lift bread and cup and remember the prisoners who cannot afford to call home, whose families cannot afford to visit, who do not have enough to eat, who cannot get the medicine they need, who sit on death row, who are afraid, who are alone. We remember you.

ALL: Remember me.

LEADER 2: We lift bread and cup and remember the prisoners because they are the members of our family who are the least of these, and when we do for the least, we do it for Christ. We know as long as we have a prison system like the one in this country that betrays all mercy and human dignity, then the night that Jesus is betrayed is every night, yet every night Jesus lifts bread and cup at the table with the betrayers, the betrayed, with friends and enemies, with the faithful and the doubtful, with prisoners and with captors, with you and with me. We remember you.

ALL: Remember me.

Prayer

LEADER 1: Come, the table is set. It's time to remember.

The Lord's Supper
GEORGE V. HUDGINS III

The Invitation

Christ came among us as a compassionate Shepherd, bringing healing and wholeness into human lives and relationships. He turned no one away from his ministry, not even those who disagreed with him, and he even shared table fellowship with the outcasts. He brought people to deeper levels of faith and wholeness within themselves, opened up new possibilities for building community, and led people into new and deeper relationships with their God. He is the Lamb of God, victorious over the evil forces of chaos.[1]

This is Christ's table. It does not belong to us. All are invited. All are welcome.

The Institution

A reading of the Institution Narrative

The Bread

The bread which we break, is it not a participation in the body of Christ?

As this bread was scattered over the mountains, and when brought together became one, so let your Church be brought together from the ends of the Earth into your Kingdom. (Didache)

The Cup

The cup of blessing which we bless, is it not a participation in the blood of Christ?

We give thanks to you, our God, for the holy vine of your servant David, which you made known to us through your child Jesus; glory to you for evermore. (Didache)

The Blessing

The pastor may pray an extemporaneous blessing of the meal, Jesus' ministry, and God's presence in the world.

Communion

The people are invited to come to a common table, or the elements are distributed to the congregation by church deacons or other congregational ministers.

The Peace

The peace of Christ be always with you.

And also with you.

Greet one another with a sign of Christ's peace.

Hymn: "Blest Be the Tie That Binds"

Blest be the tie that binds
Our hearts in Christian love;
The fellowship of kindred minds
Is like to that above.

NOTE

1. Joseph Bernardin, Morality, Peace, and Nuclear War (1996), 22: Center for Migration Studies special issues, 13: 157–165. doi:10.1111/j.2050-411X.1996.tb00129.x.

Forget about Jesus?
INEDA PEARL ADESANYA

What if the world would forget about Jesus?

Imagine that...

On this first Sunday, we commemorate Jesus' last supper
with the disciples.

We remember.
Jesus does not want us to ever forget why he came
and what he did.

He wants us to remember it as often as we can.
Particularly whenever we partake of the cup and bread
that represent his broken body and shed blood,
we remind ourselves of all that Christ sacrificed and
accomplished on our behalf.

O, praise God from whom all blessings flow and
for loving us enough to send his Son as a living sacrifice
to teach us, to lead us, and to save us!

Never alone, the Holy Spirit abides with us.

Worship, love, praise, and thank God,
and always remember what Jesus did for us on the cross!

"...do this in remembrance of me." Luke 22:19b
Hallelujah!

Communion Liturgy

ERIKA MARKSBURY

ONE: Calling God, you have gathered us
into this community.
A place has been made for us.

ALL: **Let what we say and do here
be real for us and honest to you.**

ONE: Gracious God, you have set a table before us.
To all who would come, you offer a feast.

ALL: **You hold out bread of life for all who hunger.
You hold out a cup of compassion for a broken world.**

ONE: We cannot take this bread and forget those who are
hungry.
We cannot drink this cup and forget those who thirst.

ALL: **As we feast, make our hearts restless;
stir in us a desire for justice,
so that we will not be full until all are fed.**

The Invitation Goes Out

ERIKA MARKSBURY

ONE: The invitation goes out
to all who are thirsty—

ALL: **Come, be filled.**

ONE: The invitation goes out
to all who are hungry—

ALL: **Come, be fed.**

ONE: The call comes to our ears,
an echo from ages past—

ALL: **Taste and see
that God is good.**

ONE: The song beckons us
from tomorrow—

ALL: **There is, for all,
a place at the table.**

ONE: And so we gather—
thirsty, hungry, welcome—

and we pray
that you nourish us here.

ALL: **May this bread of life**
and cup of hope
remind us of your love
for each of us
and all the world.
May they fill us
with courage and compassion
to love as you do. Amen.

Prayer after Communion
ERIKA MARKSBURY

Gracious One, having been fed at your table and
nourished by one another, send us out to feed and to
nourish the world you so love. Amen.

Benediction after Communion
JENNIFER W. DAVIDSON

Be at peace within yourself in these days ahead.
Accept that you are profoundly loved
and know in your bones
that you need never be afraid.
Be aware of the Source of Being
that is common to us all
and to all living creatures.
Be filled with the presence of the Great Compassion
toward yourself and toward all living beings.
Always be an instrument of your own liberation
and refuse to be an instrument of your own oppression.

See the face of Jesus *in* others this week.
Be the face of Jesus *for* others this week.

Be at peace within yourself
Yes, be at peace.

Amen.

Holy Communion: Some Questions
Ineda Pearl Adesanya

Consider the following as you prepare your hearts and minds to partake in Holy Communion today:

The Lord's Supper

This is my body, take eat

This is my blood, take drink

What does this symbolize ... eating and drinking?

What are we actually doing when we take communion?

Was Jesus' intent to have us to eat and drink his body and blood?

Was this to be a means of grace?

Or are we to consume and fully digest on a regular basis the purposes for which his body was broken and his blood shed?

What were/are those purposes? Redemption of sin, salvation?

What did his willingness to stay on the cross and to allow his body to be broken and his blood to be shed represent or display?

Unconditional love, sacrifice?
Willingness to suffer for us, to put our needs above his physical comfort?

Are we willing to do this for a loved one, even on a small scale?

What does it mean to sup or eat or commune together?

Why is it important for us to remember Christ in this particular way?

What did he mean that we would show forth his death until he comes again?

Is this a meant to be a perpetual reminder and representation of God's amazing grace?

Communion Prayer for Lent
JENNIFER W. DAVIDSON

God ever-giving:
You who hovered over creation,
You who birthed time itself,
And land, and sky, and sea—
From before eternity
You loved us.

You have given your people
All the things to sustain life.
In times of hunger and thirst
You provided for us.
In times of struggle,
You liberated us.
In times of our wandering
You sought us,
Forgave us
And welcomed us home.
In all our sojourns
In wilderness and desert
In city and mountain,
You promise to sustain us.

Even when we have abandoned you
You have not abandoned us.
You provide us second chances,
Pouring out your love for us
In ways beyond our imagining
Yet all so very real.

You sent Jesus, the living word
Of justice and truth
To challenge the evils of our world.
And when that world tried
To silence the living word
You challenged the very stones
To shout prophetic witness
To your glory.

And so we remember that on the night in which he was betrayed...
Continue with the words of institution.

THE CALL TO DISCIPLESHIP

Baptism and Communion as Resources for Faithful Living

> Happy are they who know that discipleship simply means the life which springs from grace, and that grace simply means discipleship.
>
> —Dietrich Bonhoeffer[1]

SAYING IT ALL AT ONCE

THE GREAT AFRICAN theologian St. Augustine expressed his frustration that it was impossible to speak of the Trinity accurately because language forces us to say only one thing at a time.[2] Although we must understand that Creator, Son, and Holy Spirit are all one thing, we can only string the words together one after another as if they were each separate things. We cannot say—or write—everything all at once! The very language we use and the persistently linear quality of words end up skewing what we most want to say.[3]

I have had a similar frustration with writing about the ordinances of baptism and communion. By necessity, we have had to deal with each of these rituals separately. Each one has its own history, its own biblical references, and its own theological treatments.

Even so, to talk about one as if it is separate from the other is to talk about each of them incompletely. Historically, baptism has been the entry point to the table. In the earliest churches, catechumenates were dismissed from worship prior to the serving of the meal. While the baptized faithful participated in Eucharist, those preparing for baptism went to classes to learn what it meant to become a follower of Christ.[4] It was only after their baptism (often at the Easter vigil, Pentecost, or Epiphany) that new Christians were able to receive communion as they were led from the baptismal pool to the table for the first time.

As discussed in chapter 9 of this book, important theological questions are raised today about whether the table should be opened to non-baptized seekers. Each congregation must grapple with how to address that question. But it is important to understand that whether baptism leads us to the meal, or the meal leads us to baptism, the two rituals were intended to go hand in hand. When we see them as two sides of the same coin, as it were, then we can begin to see that these two events are more than moments in the life of a Christian. Rather, together, they form a deep well from which we can draw to help sustain a life of discipleship drenched in grace.

DISCIPLESHIP DRENCHED IN GRACE

I want to say a word of encouragement about this idea of a life of discipleship drenched in grace. Is it really possible that these rituals stand as touchstones for lives of faithful, ongoing discipleship? Can these ordinances, these things we do occasionally during worship remind us that in all things there is grace? Can they communicate to us that everything we do is bathed in grace? Can they really remind us that God's constant invitation to us (and by us, I mean *broadly speaking*—God's invitation to *everyone, constantly extended*) is to life?

Yes. We are reminded of the gift of grace in baptism, and the invitation to life in the repeated experience of communion. At the heart of a life of discipleship is the reminder that we have nothing to fear and nothing to lose, because we lost everything in our baptism and were gifted it back in the same moment. Communion sets us again and again in that space of remembering (what some liturgical theologians call a "dangerous memory"[5]) that Jesus did not act out of his fear of what the Romans and religious leaders like us would do to him. Instead, Jesus moved faithfully in the world despite his fear, knowing his death would become his resurrection. When we are baptized and when we participate in the Lord's Supper, we participate in Jesus' death and resurrection. The astounding nature of this and the fact that it is pretty much ungraspable at any given moment are precisely why we were gifted with these two ordinances.

Jesus essentially says to us in his gift of baptism: Here, do this—let yourself experience the fear, the anxiety, and the loss of being bent over backwards so that your head goes below the surface of the water. And in that moment, know the surrender of your lives. And then, with the awareness that every breath is a gift and a miracle, let yourselves be drawn back up out of that watery tomb and take your next breath. And in this moment—and your recollection of it later—know that you have truly been set free. This is a gift to you.

And Jesus says to us in his gift of communion: Here, do this also—whenever you gather and have a meal together, remember me. Remember how I ate with outsiders, exiles, the least, the lost, and the little ones. Remember that I broke down barriers, gathered dirt and spit in it; touched mud to eyes, and hands to lips. Remember that I argued with powerful people. Remember that together we fed people even when it seemed impossible. Remember how I called people to be on this journey with me. (Remember that I didn't do all this alone!) Remember how, in everything I do, I show you who God really is, and how deeply God loves this heartbreaking, beautiful world. Remember that my hope for that world is life. And the only way to cultivate abundant, eternal life is to choose again and again to sustain it, to nurture it, to feed it. Remember when you eat the bread of life and drink the cup of suffering that you have already passed through the waters of death; you have already tasted resurrection; remember that you have nothing to fear, least of all the feast of life itself.

There is so much in our lives and our world that seeks to immerse us in the opposite message, from the moment we wake up and check our social media feed to the moment we go back to sleep at the end of yet another day filled with too much to do and too little done. We are too easily caught in a culture that pits people against one another, equates vulnerability with weakness, values grasping and greed, breeds suspicion and hatred, and urges us to hold onto what we've got and defend it at all cost.

This is why the gifts of the ordinances of baptism and communion are still so relevant and so important to the world we find ourselves living in today. We need something powerful to wake us up and keep us engaged. Baptism and communion aren't the only things that will do that. Not by any means. But when we take their theological meanings seriously, they are two things that will help sustain us for a life of faithful discipleship drenched in grace.

So why drenched in grace? The phrase *drenched in grace* is intended to convey two things. First, the visual imagery of being drenched will bring us imaginatively back to the moment of our baptism. We were sopping wet with water; yes, but also sopping with the presence of God. It doesn't matter whether you *felt* the presence of God in that water. Thank God, God's presence doesn't rely on our *feeling* God's presence.[6] Whether or not we felt it in the moment, we can be assured that God was present. More than that, just as we were drenched then, so we can assure ourselves that God is equally, abundantly present in *this* moment.

And this one.

And this.[7]

Second, despite the emphasis that believer's baptism has often been placed on an individual's decision to follow Christ, Baptists need to be reminded (perhaps more than just about any other tradition) that the whole journey of faith takes place in the context of grace. It was God's grace that ordained that we baptize at all. It is God's grace that knows that human beings need tangible, bodily, incarnational experiences of God's presence if we are to make it on this long journey of life. It is God's grace that brought us to the waters. It is in God's grace we were immersed. It is God's grace that raised us up again. It is God's grace that propels us forward to the table and the feast. It is God's grace that covers our neighbor and our enemy. It is God's grace that awaits us when we draw our dying breath.

In other words, the life of discipleship has its beginning, its middle, and its end drenched in grace. Followers of Christ, seekers of God, lovers of the Holy Spirit cannot go this journey alone. Remember, Jesus didn't either! We also cannot do it out of sheer force of will or out of the goodness of our own hearts. We will falter. We will be wrong-headed. We will get distracted by shiny things. So God brings us back to our soggy selves. And God invites us to the table at the communion supper and at every meal that's like it. God institutes these very humanlike moments that look like baths and family dinners (complete with betrayals), in order to bring us back to the inexplicable gift of grace.

MAKING THE CONNECTIONS

In this final section, we will revisit the theological themes of baptism and communion explored earlier in the book to help draw out the connections between them. In what ways do baptism and communion work together to empower our lives of discipleship?

DELIGHTING AND SUSTAINING

Both baptism and communion are meant to remind us that God takes delight in us, and that God desires that we would take delight in life. Joy and *enjoyment* are profound invitations into experiences of God's presence in our lives and in this world.

So much that surrounds us is filled with fear, anxiety, dread, and division. And there is much in the world that we must take very seriously—we must be engaged in the hard and sometimes exhausting work of justice-seeking and world-healing. But if we do this work without also taking delight in all that is astounding, beautiful, loving, and good in this world, God knows, we will only fall in a heap of despair.

Without joy, delight, and enjoyment, exhausted and discouraged disciples will do more harm than good. It is when we are overcome with fear and despair that we end up betraying and denying Jesus. But when we enter the space of resurrection, our spirits are lifted up, our lives are restored, we are nourished by God's love, and our discipleship becomes life-giving and nourishing for others as well.

DYING AND HOPING

Both baptism and communion allow us to confront the reality of death in unflinching ways. In our baptism we participate in Jesus' crucifixion—that unjust death brought about by human abuses of power, religion, and fear-fueled anger. When we observe the Lord's Supper, we remember the night in which Jesus was betrayed. It is a meal we eat with tears and a constricted throat because of what we know is to come.

But baptism and communion bring us into this direct confrontation with death not to leave us there, but to release us from its false power. The waters of baptism do not drown or bury us; they return us to life. The bread and the cup are not only the last supper held by the One to be crucified; they also point us to the first suppers with the Resurrected One on the road to Emmaus (Luke 24:13-35) and on the shores of Galilee (John 21:1-25). We participate in Jesus' death so that we might know more deeply than would be otherwise possible that *life* is the final word.

BIRTHING AND SENDING

Both baptism and communion are about God's spirit being born into God's world. The waters of baptism conjure the pain and the power of birthing pains. This is pain like no other, because it powers forth life and brings love into being. God's Spirit is constantly renewing us, calling us from comfort into challenge for the sake of God's beloved world. So, too, when we participate in communion, we allow ourselves to step into this flow of God's re-creating love for the world.

We gather around the table in the comforting presence and safety of community only to be sent out into a world that needs us. The truth is, it is also a world we need. We are called not only to be disciples of God in the world, but also to encounter Christ in that world. We will meet Christ in the least of these, in the lost, in the broken, in the silenced, in the stranger. Communion births us again into the world to be Christ for one another and to meet Christ in one another.

BELONGING AND WELCOMING

Baptism and communion are both about welcoming and belonging. We may be immersed in the waters of baptism as an individual, but when we emerge from that water, we find ourselves surrounded by fellow travelers on the way. As Khalia Jelks Williams put it, "Baptism is the moment when the community says, 'We are journeying with you.'" With water still dripping from our faces and hair, we know ourselves not only as members of the church community that surrounds us in this moment and this place, but also as members of a cosmic community that extends across space and time. We are networked through our baptism to ancestors, to those around the globe, to those who will come after us. It is more than we can ever comprehend at any given moment (Psalm 139:6).

So, too, communion will remind us that we belong to one another. Communion will try to help us feel that sense of belonging on a regular basis. We are meant to catch a glimpse of this beautiful cosmic community whenever we meet together and share the bread and cup. We may be a ragtag group, a tiny congregation of twenty people in an otherwise empty sanctuary. Or we may be one of a thousand worshipers in a sanctuary in Northeast India. Wherever we are, and however many others we see or don't see, we are gathered at one table. At this table we welcome the ones who betray and deny and fall asleep. At this table we all come as disciples in need of Jesus' welcome and presence. At this table we are profoundly reminded that we are more than one, more than individuals;

we are many, we are beloved disciples, broken and forgiven followers of Christ. We belong.

FLOODING AND CONNECTING

Baptism and communion confront us with the power of God. God's spirit is not tame; it is power-filled. We know this through the symbol of water—both life-giving and life-threatening.[8] Many of us have had to confront a very real fear of being immersed in the waters of baptism. That fear is rooted in an ancient, pre-verbal anxiety in the face of seeming chaos. Baptism forces us to give over our power, to relinquish our control, to trust that the power symbolized in the baptismal waters is ultimately loving and trustworthy.

Communion reminds us that we often fail to embody true community. When we hear the invitation to God's table, we realize that despite having experienced the power of God in our lives, we have come to rely on our own power instead. And too often we have used that power to exclude, ignore, deny, keep quiet, fight, get ahead, or undermine those whom God loves. It is okay for us to feel grief when we are confronted by communion in this way. But it is not okay for us to shut ourselves off from the grace that is offered at the same time, because that is the power of God as well. The grace of communion is the vision that the feast provides for us—the vision of a community where all are invited to thrive, to cherish one another, to sing and to dance in the presence of God's unending love. God's love is judgment for all the ways we fall short of embodying that love for one another; and God's love is mercy in all the ways it calls us back into God's grace. "You are precious in my sight, and honored, and I love you" (Isaiah 43:4).

BATHING AND REMEMBERING

Baptism and communion are public events that empower us to witness to God's intentions for the world. Baptism is a bath we take in public, because our commitment to follow Jesus is more than a private decision and greater than individual salvation. As disciples of Jesus, we take on God's heart for the world. We clothe ourselves in Christ (Romans 13:14; Colossians 3:12-17) not because we have become individually pious, but so we can be loving and compassionate members of community. We take on the qualities of kindness, humility, meekness, and patience because we need to find ways to love one another and forgive one another in our common life.

Similarly, communion is the table set in public—in the presence of our enemies, if you will. It is a meal that witnesses to the power of community in the face of forces that seek to disintegrate us. It is a meal that makes the radical claim that what is fragmented can be brought together again, can be re-membered, and made stronger than before. It is a meal that, through its dispersal, brings us together into one. It is a meal that reminds us that in giving ourselves away we will not be lost or stolen. Communion is a witness that God's way may appear like foolish weakness and vulnerability to a world hell-bent on power, but it is the only way to healing, love, and hope. Communion empowers Jesus' followers to stand together, love one another, and resist all efforts to tear the world apart.

BECOMING AND EMBODYING

Baptism and communion are identity-changing events. Through our baptisms we no longer identify as "Jew or Greek, slave or free, male or female" (Galatians 3:28). We immerse ourselves in God's mission for the world, and in doing so, we take that mission on for ourselves. We undergo a shift in our citizenship status from country to kingdom. As Marcus Pomeroy put it, when we are baptized we take a "step into a life where we are committed to feeding the hungry, visiting the sick, proclaiming liberty to the captives, and sight to the blind." This is the mission of God articulated through Jesus when he read the words of Isaiah in the synagogue (Isaiah 61:1-2; Luke 4:17-19). Participating in God's healing mission for the world is what it means to live out of our baptismal identities.

Communion is our repeated experience of inviting the life of Christ to live in us. As we eat the bread and drink from the cup, we come alive to accept the mission of Christ. Participating in the meal means we ought not leave the table unchanged. We become the Body of Christ, which is always being broken and poured out for the sake of the world that God so loves. We come alive to Christ's mission because we come alive in response to God's love. God's love surrounds us and calls us to a greater love—for God, for ourselves as beloved of God, and for one another (Mark 12:28-34, Romans 13:8-10).

SENDING FORTH

"Come to the waters," the prophet Isaiah cries out in the voice of God. "Listen carefully to me, and eat what is good, and delight yourselves in rich food" (Isaiah 55:1a, 2b). The prophet's cry reveals for us God's extravagant desire for God's beloved people to step into a life that is abundant in mercy, love, grace, and joy. Through this book we have explored together the theological themes of baptism and communion with the hope that our practices might become more robust and meaningful. Though we have discussed these ordinances one at a time, in this final chapter we have come to understand them as being intimately connected.

We have also explored some questions that arise when we engage baptism and communion in worship. These questions were not exhaustive, but will help students, pastors, and congregations begin to think through the ways our practices shape our theologies, and how our theologies likewise shape our practices. What we do in worship matters. It helps us know who God is, who we are, and how we can be more faithful disciples of Jesus in God's world.

What happens in worship is never meant to stay in worship. We are gathered together by God to become the body of Christ through our baptisms, our singing, our praying, our proclamation of Scripture and sermon, and our eating together. And then we are dispersed—sent away from this centered gathering—to be Christ *and* to meet Christ in the world. Our baptisms and the meal we share together are deep resources from which we can draw energy and life as we seek daily to embody Christ and encounter Christ. Baptism is the unique launching point into that life of discipleship, drenched in grace. Communion is the repeated experience of God's invitation into life-sustaining relationship, with God.

NOTES

1. Dietrich Bonhoeffer, *The Cost of Discipleship* (New York: Touchstone, 1995), 56.

2. Augustine, *On the Trinity* IV.21.30.

3. Stephanie Paulsell has a lovely reflection on this in her chapter "Writing as Spiritual Discipline," in *The Scope of Our Art: The Vocation of the Theological Teacher*, ed. L. Gregory Jones and Stephanie Paulsell (Grand Rapids, MI: Eerdmans, 2001), 22.

4. We have discussed this in greater detail in chapter 9 of this book.

5. See Bruce T. Morrill, S.J., *Anamnesis as Dangerous Memory: Political and Liturgical Theology in Dialogue* (Collegeville, MN: The Liturgical Press, 2000).

6. James Wm. McClendon writes: "Jesus Christ is alive; he promises his presence 'where two or three are gathered' in his name (Matthew 18:20). The Christ who brings us fully into the presence by his presence takes the initiative: we do not produce him by some liturgical conjure or evoke his memory by some spiritual stimulus; rather, we expect him as we expect a lover, a friend, an elder brother who has promised and whose promise, whose *truth* never fails." McClendon later adds, "The promise is not, 'Where two or three are gathered, you will have such and such *worship experiences*.' He only promised to be at hand." See James Wm. McClendon, *Doctrine: Systematic Theology*, vol. 2 (Nashville: Abingdon Press, 1994), 377–378 and 379.

7. And this moment, too.

8. Gordon Lathrop, *Holy Things: A Liturgical Theology* (Minneapolis: Fortress Press, 1993), 94.

QUESTIONS FOR REFLECTION AND DISCUSSION

Questions for Reflection before You Begin Reading (Baptism)

1. If you have been baptized, what (if anything) do you remember about your baptism? Do you draw on the memory of your baptism as a spiritual resource?

2. Describe a positive experience you had with baptism. Describe a negative experience.

3. Think about a promise you have made. How has that promise been significant to you or someone else? What has it meant to you to either keep or break that promise?

4. What does God do in baptism?

5. What scriptural texts come to mind first when you think about what baptism means to you?

Questions for Discussion after You Read (Baptism)

1. As you read through the different meanings of baptism, what did you identify as your home theology, your growth theology, and your journey theology?

2. Is there a theme of baptism that you read about in this section which you would like to learn more about? Discuss what attracts you or challenges you about that theology of baptism.

3. How do you understand the relationship between the individual and the community in baptism? What does it mean to say that baptism forms and reforms a community?

4. How do you think your worshiping community could incorporate remembrance and affirmation of baptism in your practices together? What difference might that make?

5. In what ways can baptism help to empower and support a life of faithful, ongoing discipleship?

Questions for Reflection before You Begin Reading (Communion)

1. What is one significant memory you have that is associated with communion? This memory can be positive or painful. Reflect on how this moment might shape your understanding of communion today.

2. Has there ever been a time in your life when you or someone you cared about struggled to receive communion? What caused the struggle?

3. What scriptural texts first come to mind when you think about what communion means to you?

4. Recall a time when Jesus shared a meal with someone in Scripture other than the Last Supper. What happened at this meal? Who was present? Who was not? What is significant about this meal?

5. Can you think of a time when a very ordinary moment became deeply meaningful for you? What happened? How do you understand God to be present in ordinary moments?

Questions for Discussion after You Read (Communion)

1. As you read through the different meanings of communion, what did you identify as your home theology, your growth theology, and your journey theology?

2. Is there a theme of communion that you read about in this section which you would like to learn more about? Discuss what attracts you or challenges you about that theology of communion.

3. How do you understand the relationship between the individual and the community in communion? In what ways do you see that relationship either made visible or obscured through your regular worship practices?

4. What does it mean to you to say: We become what we eat; we are the Body of Christ? What ramifications might this have for the ways we live in the world and how we treat ourselves and one another?

5. In what ways can communion help to empower and support a life of faithful, ongoing discipleship?

ABOUT THE CONTRIBUTORS

Rev. Ineda Pearl Adesanya, MA, MDiv, is an American Baptist–ordained minister and spiritual director. She is currently earning a PhD in Christian spirituality from the Graduate Theological Union in Berkeley, California. Ineda serves as associate minister of spiritual life for the Allen Temple Baptist Church in Oakland, California. She extends her practice part-time through teaching, pastoral counseling, and spiritual direction for the Pacific Lutheran Theological Seminary, the San Francisco Theological Seminary, the Interfaith Chaplaincy Institute, and through her public ministry, WJoy.

Sharon R. Fennema, MA, PhD, serves as the assistant professor of Christian worship and director of worship life at the Pacific School of Religion in Berkeley, California. As a liturgical scholar, practical theologian, creative worship designer, and lay member of the United Church of Christ, her teaching and research address the intersections of critical, race, postcolonial, and gender theories with embodied spiritual practices, from worship to protest, as practices which form identity and perform theology. She organizes with #interfaith4blacklives, an Oakland-based direct action solidarity group.

Rev. Tripp Hudgins, MDiv, MTS, was ordained by the American Baptist Churches USA at North Shore Baptist Church, Chicago, Illinois. Currently, Rev. Hudgins is a doctoral candidate in liturgy at the Graduate Theological Union, Berkeley, California, a postulant for the Episcopal priesthood in the Diocese of California, and a musician at All Souls Episcopal Parish.

Jean Jeffress, MDiv, is a candidate for ordination in the Northern California Nevada Conference of the United Church of Christ (NCNCUCC) and serves on the committee on ministry for the conference. Jean is a lay leader at First Congregational Church of Oakland, UCC. She is employed by Kaiser Permanente. She is also a member of Second Acts, a liturgical direct action affinity group in Oakland, California.

Erika Marksbury, MDiv, was ordained by the American Baptist Churches USA and currently serves as senior pastor of the First Baptist Church in McMinnville, Oregon. Rev. Marksbury is working toward an interdisciplinary PhD with a focus on ritual, and is a devotional writer for Illustrated Children's Ministry.

Sashinungla Pongen earned her PhD in church history at Luther Seminary, Saint Paul, Minnesota. Dr. Sashila is a member of Dimapur Ao Baptist Church (DABA), affiliated to the Nagaland Baptist Church Council (NBCC). She is an associate professor of church history at Oriental Theological Seminary in Dimapur, Nagaland, India.

Paul J. Schneider II is a lifelong American Baptist. He earned a MDiv from the American Baptist Seminary of the West and was ordained by his church of origin, the First Baptist Church of Berkeley, California, an ABCUSA church. He currently serves as pastor of Burien Community Church in Burien, Washington, an ABCUSA church in the Evergreen Association of American Baptist Churches.